POWER FOR LIVING

POWER
FOR LIVING

Commissioned by

the

Arthur S. DeMoss Foundation

to celebrate

THE YEAR OF THE BIBLE

1983

Published by

American Vision
Atlanta, Georgia

With thanks to God and in celebration

of

THE YEAR OF THE BIBLE

1983

"...*for the Word of God is powerful.*"
Heb. 4:12

*In the beginning
God created
the heavens and the earth.*
Genesis 1:1

CONTENTS

  I. SUCCESS—More Than Meets The Eye. 1

  II. THE BIBLE—What It Is And What Makes It So Special. 21

 III. HOW TO GET RIGHT WITH GOD. 41

 IV. HOW TO HANDLE LIFE'S PROBLEMS. 51

  V. HOW TO KEEP ON GROWING. 75

 VI. HOW TO READ THE BIBLE. 101

VII. GOD'S PERSPECTIVE. 119

    SUMMING IT UP. 128

    FOR FURTHER READING. 130

    ACKNOWLEDGMENTS. 132

TO THE READER

No doubt, you've heard some famous people talk about how they've found power to make their lives successful. "Why can't I have what they have?" you wondered.

Maybe it's money, fame or authority you want—things most of us, if we're really honest, crave for ourselves and those we love. Those things can be good in themselves, of course, but our *real* needs run far deeper.

You and I need truths to live by—fundamental principles that guarantee us, regardless of our present condition and circumstances, peace of mind, contentment, and purpose for vital living. Who can give these things? Only God.

"God?" you ask. "Even if He exists, how can He help me?" Throughout the history of mankind, the greatest minds have pondered that question. Answering it is the real purpose for this book. Here you'll learn what the Bible, God's love letter to the world, says about how to find solutions to every problem you'll ever encounter—personal, family, moral, business or social.

POWER FOR LIVING puts you in touch with practical ways to deal with life's challenges without being overcome or defeated.

POWER FOR LIVING shows you how to see beyond your own immediate problems and helps you put your life in perspective. It helps you apply the Bible's principles to every area of your life—your business, education and family; even the practice of science, politics, the arts, medicine and so on. This book also shows you specific ways to study the Bible so its truths make a positive, powerful difference in your life.

The Bible says God rewards those who earnestly and genuinely seek Him. You *are* a genuine seeker. **POWER FOR LIVING** is written for seekers like you—people who want real answers to the eternal questions: Who am I? Why was I created? Where am I going?

Even non-seekers, confirmed doubters, find incredible answers within the Bible at which they scoff. One man wrote, "...a strange thing happened...I began to have a thirst for the Word in the Bible I once scorned. I found myself avidly studying it. And as I did, answers to questions that had long perplexed me fell into place....I felt a new freedom within me...it was clear that all the directions I sought for life were right in this book. And then one morning it all seemed to come together as I read Psalm 119:11... *'Thy word have I hid in mine heart, that I might not sin against Thee.'*"

POWER FOR LIVING is for all who desire to know God in all His fulness. It's written for those who understand that knowing God is the first step towards knowing ourselves, our friends (and even our enemies), and the world we occupy.

God's love letter was written to you, and to all mankind. It contains prayer, praise, principles and promises. His words apply to you *right where you are*. They are more up-to-date than today's newspaper. Further, God tells us His Word will not return to Him void. Thus, through His Word—the Bible—you'll find fulfillment for your life.

Discover that love letter today. It truly offers all the power our lives will ever need!

This is what the Lord says:
"Let not the wise man boast of his wisdom
or the strong man boast of his strength
or the rich man boast of his riches,
but let him who boasts boast about this:
that he understands and knows me,
that I am the Lord, who exercises kindness,
justice and righteousness on earth,
for in these I delight,"
declares the Lord.
Jeremiah 9:23,24

SUCCESS
MORE THAN MEETS THE EYE

Everyone has his own definition of *success* and *happiness*. What makes you happy won't necessarily make someone else happy. Part of the reason for the difference is that you are a unique individual.

No one precisely like you ever existed before or will exist again. Every single human being is special and one of a kind. Still, some things are similar. Like the desire to be happy and successful.

EIGHT WHO MADE IT

The list of successful people fills *Who's Who* books. And the list is growing larger every day. In the pages ahead you'll read about eight people who have achieved the kind of success that *never* fails. As you read, think about their successes, how they were achieved, and what makes such successes important.

Then think about yourself. What qualities do you possess, or need to acquire, in order to attain your own quota of lasting success? How do your standards compare to theirs?

Remember, you too were designed to live a dynamic, successful life. The Bible shows you how! Now, brief statements from eight "superstars" who depend upon God's love letter for true **POWER FOR LIVING!**

Roger Staubach

FOOTBALL SUPERSTAR

Ours is a very dynamic, fast-paced world. Sometimes your mind seems to spin when you consider everything that is happening. It seems that it's just one thing after another, that you just can't enjoy peace of mind.

To me, there's a very simple solution. If you have a relationship with Jesus Christ, He will give you peace of mind.

My future reaches far beyond football, and this really excites me. Christianity is the most important part of my life.

If we live for God and not for ourselves, we'll be able to withstand anything in our life. If only we'd try to live beyond the simply earthly life we're involved in every day, there wouldn't be problems like war, adultery, prejudice, and crime.

> *Since we have been justified through faith, we have peace with God through our Lord Jesus Christ* (Rom. 5:1).

Charles Colson

FORMER COUNSEL
TO THE PRESIDENT OF THE UNITED STATES

I felt a strange deadness when I left the White House. I'd gotten to the top of the mountain, and I couldn't think of any other mountains.

And then I saw Tom Phillips, an old friend, a guy much like myself. By age forty, he had become president of a large corporation—a fantastic success story. When I saw him in the spring of '73, he seemed totally different—less frantic. He was smiling, he was radiant, caring about me. What had happened? He'd committed his life to Jesus Christ.

The whole idea of an intelligent, educated, successful businessman, saying, "I've accepted Him and committed my life," just threw me. Months went by. Then one evening Tom read me the chapter on pride in C. S. Lewis' *Mere Christianity*. It was a torpedo.

My biggest problem had always been intellectual reservations. I knew there was a God, but I could never see how man could have a personal relationship with Him. Then the case for Christ became obvious. That night I experienced a feeling of tremendous cleansing, of wholeness, as I accepted Jesus Christ as my Lord and Saviour.

> **The mind of sinful man is death, but the mind controlled by the Spirit is life and peace...** (Romans 8:6).

Stan Smith

PRO-TENNIS PLAYER

I haven't always been confident about my game. Before my sophomore year in college, I'd always considered myself a mediocre player. That year I met a group of athletes at the University of Southern California—guys different from what I had known before. They told me about a Person who was very new and exciting to me—Jesus Christ. Toward the end of that year, I put my life into His hands.

I asked Jesus to give my life more meaning and He did. He helped me find myself. My frustration seemed to drain off. And I felt self-confident in a way I'd never known before.

Jesus Christ helped me win over myself. It's so clear to me now why in everything, I've got to be a mirror of His teachings.

Jesus said, *"I am the light of the world. Whosoever follows me will never walk in darkness, but will have the light of life"* (John 8:12).

Wallace Johnson
CO-FOUNDER OF HOLIDAY INNS

People are important. The fellow digging the ditch is just as important as the guy who puts the roof on the house. If the guy didn't dig the ditch, the other fellow wouldn't be putting the roof on.

When there are people problems, it seems to me that the cause is a lack of the proper attitude—toward ourselves, toward God, and toward our fellow man. I've had a lot of successes and my share of trials. I've worked long and hard, often as much as sixteen hours a day, under some trying circumstances. Through them all, I've learned that the only answer to problems—and to the future of the world—is having a personal relationship with Jesus Christ. The only people who are truly happy are those who have found Jesus.

The one reason why we've always had an open Bible in every room in the Holiday Inn motels is to help people find Jesus and the solution to their problems, no matter what they are. I could reminisce about how that open Bible has saved thousands. Once, a man from Mobile, Alabama, who had had some business reversals packed a gun and drove to Birmingham with the intention of killing himself. When he checked into a Holiday Inn and found the open Bible in his room, he read it and found Christ.

Personal problems, social problems—whatever the problem—the solution is found in knowing Jesus Christ. I know He's made the difference in my life. Why not in yours?

Joe Green

DEFENSIVE LINEMAN FOR THE
PITTSBURGH STEELERS

For a long time, I thought being a good person could get me to heaven. I thought I could continue to make my own decisions, chart my own course, without the help of God. But I was also feeling the tension and pressure of trying to live my own life. I was tired, and I wanted help.

When I accepted Jesus Christ as my Saviour, I found rest, something I had never felt before. There was a peace of mind. My patience has gotten a lot better. I can sit and let the smoke clear. Before, I would be impatient, or frustration might set in, or I just would ignore problems altogether.

I feel that the things that have happened to me have happened for a reason. I'm an athlete, and I believe God has a plan for me. Whatever God leads me into, I'm confident that He will prepare me.

> *Therefore, if anyone is in Christ, he is a new creation; the old has gone, the new has come!* (II Corinthians 5:17).

Arthur S. DeMoss

INSURANCE COMPANY FOUNDER

Shortly before my twenty-fifth birthday, I was tens of thousands of dollars in debt. This in spite of the fact that I'd been working over 100 hours a week.

Like so many other businessmen, I had the peculiar notion that I was indispensable to my business. If I had to leave it for even a few hours, I'd call the office frequently just to make sure everything was all right.

When I gave my life to Jesus Christ, He promised to lift my burdens, meet all my needs, and solve my problems. He first took me out of debt right after my conversion. I no longer had to work night and day and Sundays.

What did I do? I put God first. The more time and money I gave Him, the more He gave me. Now I spend time every day reading the Bible and praying for God's guidance. I've given God my business and any problems that come up. Some might say it's incredible, but it's true; I never worry anymore.

> *Do not be anxious about anything, but in everything, by prayer and petition, with thanksgiving, present your requests to God. And the peace of God...will guard your hearts and your minds in Christ Jesus* (Philippians 4:6, 7).

Edward L. Johnson

RESPECTED VOICE OF THE FINANCIAL INDUSTRY

As Chief Executive Officer of Financial Federation, Inc., I had to determine what was good and what was bad for the business. I felt the responsibility for handling two and one half billion dollars in total assets and one hundred sixty million dollars in stock holder's equity. That demanded uncompromising standards and all the business acumen I had.

I didn't go around waving a flag, but I made no bones about it—I sought and received God's help in my business. Success, for me, means being in the will of God. That's the kind of success which is eternal—not subject to the whims of a changing economy. The Scriptures say that the one who does the will of God abides forever. I believe that and I live by that.

One of the things that made an impact on my life was when someone said to me, "Your mother prayed for you before you were born." She died when I was only three, and I committed my life to Christ when I was seventeen. I've gone on and trusted the Lord ever since. His help is a constant reality in every facet of my life: at home, in church, in sorrow, in joy. Why shouldn't it work in business?

> *I want those already wise to become the wiser and become leaders by exploring the depths of meaning in these nuggets of truth.* (Proverbs 1:5,6).

Julius "Dr. J." Erving

NBA BASKETBALL STAR AND
1981 NBA MOST VALUABLE PLAYER

At age twenty-nine I realized that I was looking good on the outside but was hitting a lot of peaks and valleys on the inside. After searching for the meaning of life for over ten years, I found the meaning in Jesus Christ.

When I gave my life to Jesus Christ, I began to understand my true purpose for being here. It's not to go through life and experience as many things as you possibly can and then turn to dust and be no more. The purposes in life are to be found through having Christ in your life and understanding what His plan is and following that plan.

Now, there's no pressure in my life, and I'm never alone. I know that my Christian faith has helped me put my priorities in order. If I put God number one and my family after that, along with my social existence and my job, I can withstand any attack, any criticism.

Since I asked Christ to be my Lord and Saviour, there are still some peaks and valleys, but I am being operated on by the greatest Doctor of all time, so all the glory goes to Him.

> *Being confident of this, that he who began a good work in you will carry it on to completion until the day of Christ Jesus* (Philippians 1:6).

After reading about some of the successful people in this chapter, you may be thinking, "Well, that's *their* story. Maybe they've been lucky to get where they are."

On the other hand, perhaps, you noted things these eight individuals hold in common: a personal relationship to Jesus Christ and a profound respect for the Bible.

Why the strong attraction to the Bible and to Jesus Christ? Why should you know more about them? How can you profit from them?

You'll find life-changing answers to these questions throughout this book. If you're seeking more power for living, you'll find it. You'll find it *here*, in a way that will change you forever.

...the fruit of the Spirit
is love, joy, peace, patience, kindness,
goodness, faithfulness, gentleness
and self-control...
Galatians 5:22, 23

THE BIBLE
WHAT IT IS AND WHAT MAKES IT SO SPECIAL

Perhaps you find yourself in one of these categories:
• Someone who has heard about the Bible but never read it
• Someone who has browsed through the Bible and never understood it
• Someone who has studied the Bible but never found it helpful for today

Whatever the case, you need to know that the Bible is unique. By definition, *unique* means "one of a kind." In no other set of writings does the word *unique* so perfectly apply as to the Bible, *the* Book.

The Bible is God revealing Himself to mankind. God came to earth to show who He is—and He really did this in our history. God showed us who He is in the historical life of Jesus Christ.

That same Jesus, who came to reveal His Father to us, reveals Himself within the lives of countless numbers of "ordinary" people around us. Perhaps you remember one of them—a middle-aged man, unmarried, at first anonymous—who helped five plane crash victims escape the freezing waters of the Potomac River before he himself perished.

Few American television viewers will ever forget the compassionate stranger, who on January 13, 1982, selflessly exemplified the words of Jesus Christ: *"Greater love has no man than this, that a man lay down his life for his friends"* (John 15:13).

CLEARING THE DUST OFF

Some people have antiques inherited from previous generations. Though these items may be valuable, sometimes they are considered mere "dust catchers." Many valuable artifacts are placed on a shelf or packed away: though they may be priceless, they possess little practical value. No one uses them.

Because the Bible has been handed down through many centuries, some people think it's an antique. To them, it's only potentially valuable—or perhaps worth nothing at all! Let's dust off everything that obscures our vision and clouds our understanding of the Bible's real message—a message that's timely, that's fresh, that's for *you.*

THE BEGINNING

The Bible was written over a *period of about fifteen hundred years* (from around 1440 B.C. to around A.D. 90) by more than forty authors from every walk of life including kings, peasants, poets, fishermen, statesmen, and scholars.

The Bible was written *in different places.* Moses, the great political leader and recipient of God's law, wrote his books in a desert. Luke, a medical doctor, wrote while traveling with the Apostle (missionary) Paul. Paul wrote much of the New Testament while in prison; they were letters to Christians in different countries. During war and peace, in the midst of great joy or from the depths of great sorrow, God had His Word written. The Bible was written *on three continents:* Asia, Africa, and Europe. And it was written in *three languages:* Hebrew (the language of the Jewish people), Aramaic (the common language of the Near East until the time of Alexander the Great), and Greek (the international language at the time of Christ).

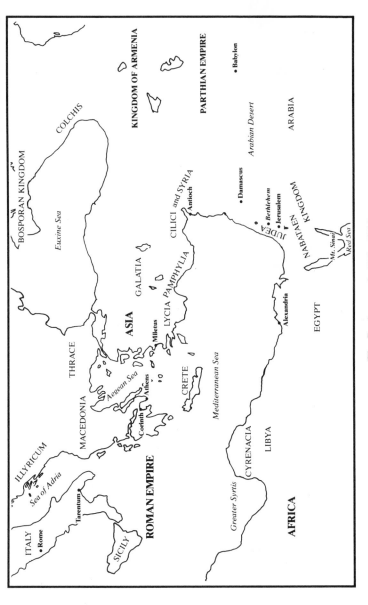

The Background of The Bible

The Bible is divided *into two main parts:* The Old Testament and the New Testament. The word *testament* as used in the Bible means covenant, *an oath that God sovereignly makes with His people.*

One of the main themes of the Bible, in both the Old and New Testaments, is God's ongoing covenant or agreement with His people. In the Old Testament, God promised to bless those who were brought into a living relationship with Him and remained faithful to the covenant requirements.

Through the years God sought to deepen His people's understanding of their covenant relationship to Him. Conformity to a standard of behavior as summarized in the Ten Commandments was the heart of the "old" covenant. In the book of Jeremiah, chapter 31, verses 31 through 34, we see God keeping His covenant and adding a new dimension to it. God will deal with the heart and mind of His children in a fuller and deeper way:

> *"The time is coming" declares the LORD, "when I will make a new covenant...I will put my law in their minds and write it on their hearts...I will be their God, and they will be my people...they will all know me" ...declared the LORD.*

That new covenant or agreement was established with the coming of Jesus Christ, through His life, death, resurrection from the dead, and ascension into heaven. Jesus Christ fulfilled all the requirements for righteous living laid down in the Old Testament. What we as sinners could not do because of our disobedience, Jesus accomplished through His obedience. The power to fulfill the dictates of God's requirements is made possible through the outpouring of God's Spirit in the lives of those who believe. The Holy Spirit is the Presence of God operating in the world within each person who is brought into a relationship with God through Jesus Christ.

> *And God said,*
> *"This is the sign of the covenant*
> *I am making between me and you*
> *and every living creature with you,*
> *a covenant for*
> *all generations to come:*
> *I have set my rainbow*
> *in the clouds,*
> *and it will be*
> *the sign of the covenant*
> *between me and the earth.*
> *Whenever I bring clouds over the earth*
> *and the rainbow appears in the clouds,*
> *I will remember my covenant*
> *between me and you and*
> *all living creatures of every kind.*
> *Never again will the waters*
> *become a flood to destroy life.*
> Genesis 9:12-15

Such people are individuals who entered into a personal relationship with Jesus Christ and made a covenant, pledge, or agreement with God. They willingly tell of His presence in their lives and speak of Him at work, in newspaper stories, sportscasts, kitchens, and college campuses.

These people believe the Bible must be central to any successful lifestyle within today's tumultuous world. One of them, a President, proclaimed 1983 as *The Year of the Bible.*

This new life in Christ is not just for Presidents, but for *all* who believe. From the first book of the Bible (Genesis) to the last book of the Bible (Revelation) there is one unfolding and unifying theme—God saving His people from their sins.

A BOOK THAT ENDURES

One of the unique aspects of the Bible is its endurance, its ability to survive the attacks of those who seek to destroy its message and influence. It has survived through time because it's God's *Word.* Because it is God's Word we should expect it to survive no matter how often its claims are ridiculed or its demands ignored.

Kathryn Koob, an American diplomat who spent 444 days as a hostage in Iran, told her guards, "We may be here for the next fifteen years! And my job is to sit here and wait."

Before the eyes of individuals hostile to the faith common in the land of her fathers, Kathryn Koob set out to establish a meaningful system of morning disciplines—Bible study, prayer and meditation, and reading.

"They couldn't believe I could take that attitude," she said. Despite screams outside that would continue until two in the morning, then begin again at six a.m., an American political prisoner found peace in the midst of mob hatred—*courage* and *peace,* from the Bible!

The Bible has withstood violent attacks from its enemies. It has been banned, burned, and outlawed at various times by various individuals and groups of people.

Voltaire, the famous French atheist who died in 1778, said the Bible and Christian faith would not be believed in one hundred years. On the 100th anniversary of his statement, the Geneva Bible Society purchased Voltaire's printing press and house and started to print Bibles from there. Voltaire is dead but the Bible continues to make its impact on the world: ***"The grass withers and the flowers fall, but the word of our God stands forever"*** (Isaiah 40:8).

MAKING AN IMPACT

"The patience of Job," "a doubting Thomas," "being a Good Samaritan," "having the wisdom of Solomon," and "an eye for an eye" are phrases probably familiar to many people. They happen to come from the Bible. Did you know what a deep impact the Bible has made on Western civilization and on our society in particular?

ON LAW AND GOVERNMENT

It's no accident the similarities between modern law and biblical law are quite striking. What the two have in common are:
- seeking justice
- operating on the basis of impartiality
- giving legal protection to the innocent.

Even the idea of meting out different types of punishment to suit a crime comes from the Bible.

Every time you pick up a United States coin,—penny, nickel, dime, or quarter—you hold in your hand evidence of the tremendous impact of the Bible on our country—"In

God We Trust." That impact did not come by chance.

When October 12 occurs each year, few of us recall that it's the birthday of Christopher Columbus. School children commemorate this day, but how many realize the Bible's influence on the man whose life so significantly shaped the course of world events? From Columbus' *Book of Prophecies* come these words:

> It was the Lord who put it into my mind—I could feel His hand upon me—the fact that it could be possible to sail from here to the Indies... All who heard of my project rejected it with laughter, ridiculing me... There is no question that the inspiration was from the Holy Spirit, because He comforted me with rays of marvelous illumination from the Holy Scriptures.

Many of the Founding Fathers of this country lived by the principles and truths of the Bible. Even those who were not Christians continued to respect the truths of the Bible.

> The longer I live, the more convincing proofs I see of this truth, that God governs in the affairs of men. And if a sparrow cannot fall to the ground without His notice, is it probable that an empire can rise without His aid?

These words were spoken by Benjamin Franklin at the Constitutional Convention of 1787. The Bible was his source book as he addressed George Washington and the other men who had gathered to draft a new governing document for the thirteen independent states. In that same speech he went on to say:

> We have been assured, sir, in the sacred writings, that ***"except the Lord build the house, they labor in vain that build it."*** I firmly believe this and I also believe that, without His concurring aid, we shall succeed in this political building no better than the builders of Babel ...And, what is worse, mankind may hereafter...

despair of establishing government by human wisdom and leave it to chance, war and conquest...

Other national leaders followed Franklin's example in turning to the Bible to help shape the nation. George Washington, our nation's first President said, "It is impossible to rightly govern the world without God and the Bible."

On March 30, 1883, President Abraham Lincoln appointed a "National Fast Day." In it he said:

> We have been preserved these many years in peace and prosperity. We have grown in numbers, wealth and power as no other nation has ever grown. But we have forgotten God. We have forgotten the gracious hand which has preserved us in peace, and multiplied and enriched and strengthened us....

Lincoln's words have a 20th-century up-to-dateness about them:

> We have vainly imagined, in the deceitfulness of our hearts, that all these blessings were produced by some superior wisdom and virtue of our own. Intoxicated with unbroken success, we have become too self-sufficient to feel the necessity of redeeming and preserving grace, too proud to pray to the God that made us.

On another occasion, President Lincoln stated that he believed "the Bible is the best gift God has ever given to men. All the good from the Saviour of the world is communicated to us through this book."

Even the walls of our government buildings bear testimony to the centrality of the Bible in American life:

- The Ten Commandments hang over the head of the Chief Justice of the Supreme Court.

- In the House and Senate chambers appear the words, "In God we Trust."

- In the Rotunda is the figure of the crucified Christ.
- On the walls of the Capitol dome, these words appear: "The New Testament according to the Lord and Saviour Jesus Christ."
- On the Great Seal of the United States is inscribed the phrase *Annuit Coeptis,* "God has smiled on our undertaking." Under the Seal is the phrase from Lincoln's immortal Gettysburg Address: "This nation under God."

Noah Webster, author of the *American Dictionary of the English Language* (1828), makes the following statement that captures the Bible's influence in the development of our great nation:

> The moral principles and precepts contained in the scriptures ought to form the basis of all our civil constitutions and laws. All the miseries and evils which men suffer from vice, crime, ambition, injustice, oppression, slavery, and war, proceed from their despising or neglecting the precepts contained in the Bible.

The origin and foundation of America and her free form of civil government spring from a deeply held commitment to the Bible.

ON LITERATURE AND THE ARTS

Law and government have been influenced by the Bible as well as literature and the arts. Bible characters, illustrations, themes, and sayings have all found their way into popular speech and writings. "Turn the other cheek," "Spare the rod, and spoil the child," and "A house divided against itself must fall" are common expressions taken from the Bible.

Knowledge of the Bible is indispensable for the reader who desires to understand Dante's *Divine Comedy,* Milton's

Paradise Lost or Bunyan's *Pilgrim's Progress.* These are but a sample of the list of writers and poets who claimed the Bible as the source of inspiration for their life and writings, or who have been influenced by ideas from the Bible:

Alexander Solzhenitsyn
C. S. Lewis
J. R. R. Tolkien
T. S. Eliot
Fedor Dostoevski
Dorothy Sayers
Malcolm Muggeridge
Flannery O'Connor
Noah Webster
Daniel Webster
Robert Louis Stevenson
William Shakespeare
Emily Dickinson
Herman Melville
Daniel Defoe

A complete list would run for pages. And we haven't mentioned artists and musicians influenced by themes in the Bible, such names as Bach, Handel, Mendelssohn, Reubens, Rouault, DaVinci, Dore...

ON SCIENCE

Whenever we drop something, it eventually must land on the ground or fall toward the earth. That's something which can be repeated time after time, a force that has been given the status of a LAW—the Law of Gravity. Without that predictable law, our bodies and other objects would drift off into space.

You probably know about the Law of Gravity, but do you know who explained it in terms of the Bible? Isaac

Newton, considered to be the *most important* scientist prior to the 20th century.

Newton was the first person to develop a comprehensive science of the physical world. He developed the mathematical system called Calculus. He also discovered basic laws of motion for the universe, as well as the basic principles of color and sight.

Isaac Newton was no average scientist. Thanks to him, science has been enriched. But who was he and what did he believe?

First of all, Isaac Newton saw predictable principles operating in the created order. He credited these principles to the God of the Bible:

> Without all doubt, this world . . . could arise from nothing but the perfectly free will of God. . . .From this fountain. . . .what we call the laws of nature have flowed . . . These therefore we must not seek from uncertain conjectures, but learn from observations and experiments.

As brilliant as Newton was, he believed it presumptuous to suppose man could "find the true principles of physics and the laws of natural things by the force alone of his own mind and the internal light of reason."

Why could Newton say we can "learn from observations and experiments?" Because he knew the Bible speaks of an orderly creation, not a haphazard collection of random events.

The created order can be studied and cultivated to bring forth its God-ordained potential, all for the glory of God and the advancement of His kingdom. This includes agriculture, astronomy, engineering, architecture, navigation, medicine, biology, science, aviation, physics, music, industry, education, horticulture, athletics, economics, politics, health, law, and every other conceivable creative endeavor.

For example, Wilbur and Orville Wright had to understand and obey atmospheric laws in order to take dominion over the sky. Mechanical, mathematical, and aerodynamic laws had to be studied as well, to invent an apparatus that could overcome gravity's effects. Those who wish to work with God's creation must do so in terms of His laws, both moral and natural.

It's interesting to note that the Wright brothers refused to demonstrate their flying machine on the Lord's Day, no matter who was doing the persuading.

George Washington Carver's study of chemical and agricultural laws allowed him to develop the potential of the created order that brought economic prosperity to the world. The results of his studies, in using God's laws, led to the development of innumerable products from the peanut.

Carver based his scientific study of the created order on Genesis 1:29: *"I give you every seed-bearing plant on the face of the whole earth and every tree that has fruit with seed in it. They shall be yours for food."* George Washington Carver devoutly believed that "a personal relationship with the Creator of all things was the only foundation for the abundant life." His words tell the whole story:

> I carried the peanuts into my laboratory and the Creator told me to take them apart and resolve them into their elements. With such knowledge as I had of chemistry and physics I set to work to take them apart. I separated the water, the fats, the oils, the gums, the resins, sugars, starches, pectoses, pentosans, amino acids. There! I had the parts of the peanuts all spread out before me (Rackham Holt, *George Washington Carver: An American Biography*, pp. 226-227).

From this seemingly insignificant legume he made cheese, milk, flour, ink, dyes, wood stains, and soap, to list but a few of his nearly 300 derivative products.

The list of scientists who looked to the Bible as the foundation for all truth includes Kepler, Pascal, Kelvin, Faraday, Pasteur, Linnaeus, Mendel, Maxwell, and many other great scientists of the past and present.

During the final chaotic days of Hitler's Third Reich, several young German scientists met secretly by night—to pray. Their mission? To learn where God would have them flee, before Germany fell to the approaching allied armies. As research and development geniuses in the world's foremost new frontier— space exploration—they knew their expertise literally would determine the future of this entire planet.

Russia or the U.S.A.? Some of them hoped to remain in Europe; America seemed hopelessly alien and far from home. Eventually, the U.S.A. won that strange and secret ballot. The Germans voted to bring their awesome knowledge to the nation *under God,* a nation undergirded by the Bible.

Thus God led Dr. Werner von Braun to America, to put our space program into orbit. Later he explained that he could not take God's scientific principles to Russia—a country dedicated to suppressing all religion, and especially the Bible.

———————————

In previous pages you read about the Bible's influence on our culture, as well as the beliefs of some of our most important thinkers. But, what does the Bible say about itself? While it's interesting to know what man says about God's Word, it's *important* to know what God says!

WHAT THE BIBLE SAYS ABOUT ITSELF

The Bible claims to be the Word of God. No other book makes such an authoritative claim about itself. Nearly 4,000 times in the first section of the Bible—the Old Testament— you will find words like "the Lord spoke," "the Word of the Lord," "the Lord commanded," "God spoke all these words," and so on. The New Testament says, *"All Scripture is God-breathed and is useful for teaching, rebuking, correcting and training in righteousness"* (2 Timothy 3:16).

Although God used men, this verse says *"Scripture is God-breathed."* The Bible owes its origin and contents to God. The human authors were powerfully guided and directed by the Holy Spirit. This makes the Bible different from all other books written by men.

George Frederick Handel's inspiration for the famed oratorio *Messiah* was taken from the Bible. After completing the soaringly magnificent "Hallelujah Chorus" Handel was deeply stirred by its message. He saw Jesus Christ in all His glory, power, and majesty. Handel's oratorio has affected millions of other worshippers since it was first performed.

You might be moved to write a great book, poem, or even a song, but your inspiration would come from within. Not so with the Bible, whose source of inspiration is God Himself. When God decided to reveal Himself, Scripture began. When He had finished revealing Himself with the last book of the Bible, Scripture ended. All of this is true because the words of the Bible, down to the letters themselves (Matthew 5:18), originated in God and not in man.

The Bible is not only God's Word to man, it is God's *only* Word to man. We don't have to sort through a hundred

In the beginning was the Word,
and the Word was with God,
and the Word was God.
He was with God in the beginning.
John 1:1,2

and one other voices which claim to be God's Word. We don't have to stumble through life, wondering if God has anything to say to us. He had already spoken to us in the Bible. It is the only map to life that correctly guides us.

A certain soft drink advertises itself as "the real thing." The Bible is "the real thing"when it comes to communication from God. He has not given us an assortment of words from which we can choose. There is only one Word from God.

Whatever God says is binding on the world. His words cannot be taken back. His words cannot be nullified by the words of skeptics or the decrees of political leaders.

The Bible is one Word. It cannnot be chopped up. It must be viewed as a whole because it is *one* Word. The Bible is also one in that the message is the same from beginning to end. The message is as broad as all sixty-six books, or it is as narrow as one Word. That one Word is Jesus.

The Gospel of John begins: ***"In the beginning was the Word, and the Word was with God, and the Word was God. He was with God in the beginning... The Word became flesh and lived for a while among us"*** (John 1:1, 2, 14). The *Word* mentioned here refers to Jesus Christ, God's final means of communicating with the world. Jesus Christ is the same Word who called the universe into existence, who gave us commandments to live by, and redeemed His people through His sinless life and shed blood. So everything—nature, law, and salvation—is governed by the Word of God.

Such power and authority governs every area of life. Scripture is the final authority for everything and everyone. Eric Liddell (the central figure in the recent film *Chariots of Fire*) was challenged by the royalty of England because during the 1924 Olympic Games he refused to participate in the 100 meter dash because the event was to be run on Sunday. Liddell believed God's Word said man should work six days and worship and rest one day. An English nobleman who took exception to Liddell's beliefs said, "If you were a Christian, you would run for your country." To that, Liddell responded, "God created the rules that nations are to be run by."

The fact that many do not believe that the Bible is God's authoritative Word does not change its message or nullify its authority. God's Word will last forever even when everything else has long ceased to exist.

The Bible unfolds a history that is the most important history we know. That's because it is not primarily a record of men! It is the record of what God did in our history. That's why the Bible is so encouraging. God is the central figure. He is the subject of all the activity.

But, why read the Bible?

When we read history books or listen to the evening news, we can't help but think, "People keep making the same mistakes over and over again. When will they learn?"

The Bible says no one ever will learn on his own.

Murder, wars, injustice, deception, jealousy, envy, anger, depression, drunkenness, adultery—these are some of the things we find in the world. Even with the greatest minds working at solving these problems, humankind remains incapable of pulling itself out of the muck. Why?

All the things that keep the world on the brink of disaster result from sin—another word for rebellion against God.

Only when people get right with God through Jesus Christ will our families, schools, businesses, churches, and nation fully understand what true power for living is all about.

"How do I get right with God?" is the most important question you could ask yourself. The all-important answer is found in the following chapter.

*I tell you the truth,
whoever hears my word and
believes him who sent me
has eternal life
and will not be condemned;
he has crossed over
from death to life.*
John 5:24

*If you declare with your lips
"Jesus is Lord,"
and believe in your heart
that God raised him from the d
You will be saved.
For we believe in our heart;
and are put right with God,
we declare with our lips
and are saved.*
Romans 10: 9,10

HOW TO GET
RIGHT
WITH GOD

Ask yourself: What one thing do I want above everything else in the world? You want *life!* And that's just what our Lord promised us when He said, ***"I am come that they might have life, and have it more abundantly"*** (John 10:10).

There is a Book that points us toward the Author and Giver of all life. "There is a Book," Patrick Henry declared, "worth all other books which were ever printed."

Napoleon, while on St. Helena, said, "The Gospel is not merely a book—it is a living power—a book surpassing all others...The soul can never go astray with this book for its guide."

Life! The Bible exudes life, with all its fulness, abundance and power. The Bible can shine light from its pages into the darkest corner of any heart, yet Thomas Adams, a 19th-century American economist, saw fit to warn:

> The Bible is to us what the star was to the wise men; but if we spend all our time in gazing upon it, observing its motions, and admiring its splendor, without being led to Christ by it, the use of it will be lost to us.

How do you find Christ through the pages of God's Word? How can you come into intimate fellowship with the Lord God of our universe? How do you even begin to read that Love Letter He composed for us all, before the foundation of the world?

The Bible answers all these wonderful questions, plus many, many others that crowd into your heart. To begin, let's consider God's spiritual laws.

Just as there are physical laws that govern the physical universe, so are there spiritual laws which govern your relationship with God.

LAW ONE

GOD LOVES YOU AND OFFERS A WONDERFUL PLAN FOR YOUR LIFE.

GOD'S LOVE
"For God so loved the world, that He gave His only begotten Son, that whoever believes in Him should not perish, but have eternal life" (John 3:16).

GOD'S PLAN
(Christ is speaking): *"I came that they might have life, and might have it abundantly"* (that it might be full and meaningful) (John 10:10).

Why is it that most people are not experiencing the abundant life?

Because...

LAW TWO

MAN IS SINFUL AND SEPARATED FROM GOD. THEREFORE, HE CANNOT KNOW AND EXPERIENCE GOD'S LOVE AND PLAN FOR HIS LIFE.

MAN IS SINFUL
"For all have sinned and fall short of the glory of God" (Romans 3:23).

Man was created to have fellowship with God; but, because of his stubborn self-will, he chose to go his own independent way and fellowship with God was broken. This self-will, characterized by an attitude of active rebellion or passive indifference, is evidence of what the Bible calls *sin.*

MAN IS SEPARATED
"For the wages of sin is death" (Romans 6:23).

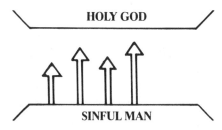

This diagram illustrates that God is holy and man is sinful. A great gulf separates the two. The arrows illustrate that man continually tries to reach God and the abundant life through his own efforts, such as a good life, philosophy or religion. The third law explains the only way we can bridge this gulf...

LAW THREE

JESUS CHRIST IS GOD'S ONLY PROVISION FOR MAN'S SIN. THROUGH HIM YOU CAN KNOW AND EXPERIENCE GOD'S LOVE AND PLAN FOR YOUR LIFE.

HE DIED IN OUR PLACE
"But God demonstrates His own love toward us, in that while we were yet sinners, Christ died for us" (Romans 5:8).

HE ROSE FROM THE DEAD
"Christ died for our sins...He was buried...He was raised on the third day, according to the Scriptures ...He appeared to Peter, then to the twelve. After that He appeared to more than five hundred..."
(I Corinthians 15:3-6).

HE IS THE ONLY WAY TO GOD
"Jesus said to him, 'I am the way, and the truth, and the life; no one comes to the Father, but through Me'"
(John 14:6).

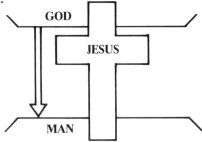

This diagram illustrates that God has bridged the gulf which separates us from Him by sending His Son, Jesus Christ, to die on the cross in our place to pay the penalty for our sins. But it is not enough to know these three laws. We also need to know:

LAW FOUR

WE MUST INDIVIDUALLY RECEIVE JESUS CHRIST AS SAVIOUR AND LORD; THEN WE CAN KNOW AND EXPERIENCE GOD'S LOVE AND PLAN FOR OUR LIVES.

WE MUST RECEIVE CHRIST
"But as many as received Him, to them He gave the right to become children of God, even to those who believe in His name" (John 1:12).

WE RECEIVE CHRIST THROUGH FAITH
"For by grace you have been saved through faith; and that not of yourselves, it is the gift of God; not as a result of works, that no one should boast" (Ephesians 2:8,9).

WHEN WE RECEIVE CHRIST, WE EXPERIENCE A NEW BIRTH (Read John 3:1-8).

WE RECEIVE CHRIST BY PERSONAL INVITATION
(Christ is speaking): *"Behold, I stand at the door and knock; if any one hears My voice and opens the door, I will come in to him"* (Revelation 3:20).

Receiving Christ involves turning to God from self (repentance) and trusting Christ to come into our lives to forgive our sins and to make us the kind of people He wants us to be. It's not enough just to agree intellectually that Jesus Christ is the Son of God and that He died on the cross for our sins. Nor is it enough to have only an emotional experience. We receive Jesus Christ by faith, as an act of the will.

These two circles represent two kinds of lives:

SELF-DIRECTED LIFE

S— Self is on the throne

+ — Christ is outside

• — interests are directed by self, often resulting in discord and frustration

CHRIST-DIRECTED LIFE

+ — Christ is in the life and on the throne

S — Self is yielding to Christ

• — interests are directed by Christ, resulting in harmony with God's plan

Which circle best represents your life?

Which circle would you like to have represent your life?

The following explains how you can receive Christ:

YOU CAN RECEIVE CHRIST BY FAITH THROUGH PRAYER
(Prayer is talking with God)

God knows your heart and is not so concerned with your words as He is with the attitude of your heart. The following is a suggested prayer:

"Lord Jesus, I need You. Thank You for dying on the cross for my sins. I open the door of my life and receive You as my Saviour and Lord. Thank You for forgiving my sins and giving me eternal life. Take control of the throne of my life. Make me the kind of person You want me to be." Does this prayer express the desire of your heart? If it does, pray this prayer right now, and Christ will come into your life, as He promised.

HOW TO KNOW THAT CHRIST IS IN YOUR LIFE

Did you receive Christ into your life? According to His promise in Revelation 3:20, where is Christ right now in relation to you? Christ said that He would come into your life. Would He mislead you? On what authority do you know that God has answered your prayer?

(The trustworthiness of God Himself and His Word!)

THE BIBLE PROMISES ETERNAL LIFE TO ALL WHO RECEIVE CHRIST

And the witness is this, that God has given us eternal life, and this life is in His Son. He who has the Son has the life; he who does not have the Son of God does not have the life. These things I have written to you who believe in the name of the Son of God, in order that you may know that you have eternal life (1 John 5:11-13).

Thank God often that Christ is in your life and that He will never leave you (Hebrews 13:5). You can know on the basis of His promise that Christ lives in you and that you have eternal life, from the very moment you invite Him in. He will not deceive you.

An important reminder...
DO NOT DEPEND UPON FEELINGS

Our authority comes from the promise of God's Word, the Bible—*not our human feelings.* The Christian lives by total faith (trust) in God and His Word. This train diagram illustrates the relationship between *fact* (God and His Word), *faith* (our trust in God and His Word), and *feeling* (the result of our faith and obedience) (John 14:21).

The train can run *with* or *without* the caboose. It's useless, however, to attempt to *pull* the train by the caboose. As Christians, we don't depend on our feelings or emotions, which can be unreliable, but place our faith (trust) in the unfailing trustworthiness of God and the promises of His Word the Bible.

NOW THAT YOU HAVE RECEIVED CHRIST

The moment you received Christ by faith, as an act of the will, many things happened, including these:

1. Christ came into your life (Revelation 3:20 and Colossians 1:27).
2. Your sins were forgiven (Colossians 1:14).
3. You became a child of God (John 1:12).
4. You received eternal life (John 5:24).
5. You began the great adventure for which God created you (John 10:10; II Corinthians 5:17 and I Thessalonians 5:18).

Can you think of anything you could receive that would be more wonderful than Jesus Christ? Why not thank God right now in prayer, praising Him for all He does for you? By thanking God, you demonstrate your faith. Such acts of faith help you grow spiritually.

Also, you might wish to recap the four magnificent laws that can help you and all mankind get right with God. Why not list these statements on cards, and review them regularly? You'll want to know them by heart. Through these laws, you'll help others come to know them by heart. Through these laws, you'll help others come to know God's heart.

1. God loves you and offers a wonderful plan for your life.
2. Man is sinful and separated from God. Therefore, he cannot know and experience God's love and plan for his life.
3. Jesus Christ is God's only provision for man's sin. Through Him you can know and experience God's love and plan for your life.
4. We must individually receive Jesus Christ as Saviour and Lord; then we can know and experience God's love and plan for our lives.

Because you want *life,* you will come to know the Bible. Like David Livingstone, who journeyed deep into Africa, you someday may confess:

> "All that I am I owe to Jesus Christ,
> revealed to me in His divine book."

May it become *your* divine Book, also.

*Trust in the Lord with all your heart
and lean not on your own understanding;
in all your ways acknowledge him,
and he will make your paths straight.*
Proverbs 3: 5,6

ANDLE
E'S
LEMS

child threatened you or tried to
n, how did you react? If you were
led, "Stop! I'll tell my daddy (or
added, "My daddy (or mommy) is
bigger than you

As an adult, you wish your problems might be so easily solved. These days they're adult-size and maybe *feel* king-size—haunting, lingering dilemmas, frustrations, fears of every sort—the sort that produce pain and depression. You need real solutions to the kinds of trials you face on the job, at home, wherever your life leads you.

How do you handle problems?

Some people, feeling overwhelmed, withdraw from society, friends and family and simply curl into a cocoon. Others lash out, harming themselves and others around them. Still others, ostrich-like in their response, calmly deny their problems exist, managing to kid themselves and even their closest associates.

Then there are the people who face their problems openly and honestly. They know that trials, difficulties and tragedy occur in all lives, and they're prepared to deal constructively with personal misfortunes. They see themselves as overcomers.

The president of a famous technical school said, "We don't just build engineers. Every man we graduate must become a *problem-solver.*"

The Bible provides positive ways to face and overcome problems. It shows a general pattern, as well as particular guidelines, for problem-solving.

In this magnificent guidebook, you'll encounter answers to any question or dilemma your life will ever pose. The Bible offers answers to our practical needs: *building a home or a business,* principles for monetary increase, using our time wisely, learning to delegate authority.

The Bible helps meet your emotional needs, also, offering aids for loneliness, fear, uncertainty, lack of wisdom, inability to forgive, temptation—the entire catalogue of helps for the hurting human heart.

Turn to the Bible when you need tested, proven, absolutely infallible advice and guidance. **POWER FOR LIVING** includes power for living *with* problems, difficulties, or even heartbreak. How do you lay hold of that power?

"Do you read the Bible every day?" one businessman asked another.

"No."

"Then start right now" his friend encouraged. "You eat every day, sleep every night, even take vitamins daily— and your muscles begin to deteriorate in three days without exercise.

"Your spiritual health follows the same law," he continued. "If you don't stay close to the Bible, you'll get spiritually flabby within three days. If a problem crops up, you'll have no spiritual power with which to meet it."

Whether you have just become a Christian, or have lived for years as a Christian without ammunition—a Christian who does not know or use the Bible—the following pages in this book will interest you. Through the Bible, you'll receive power for living.

When a person becomes a Christian, a follower of Jesus Christ, he literally becomes a son or daughter of God, with all the benefits of that new way of living as God's child. The Holy Spirit of God begins to add power to his everyday life, giving him a picture of what heaven is like. The fruits of God's Spirit—love, peace, joy, patience, self-control, and so on—become real in his life.

As a Christian, you'll find some things that used to occupy your time no longer hold the same attraction. Your frame of reference has changed. It's as if everyone in the world is wearing dark glasses to see the sun and you've suddenly taken yours off. And how much better everything looks without the glasses!

In growing as a Christian, you may suddenly find yourself doing battle with an unseen enemy—Satan. After all, Satan, the great deceiver, doesn't like the fact that you've turned your back on him. He's lost a valuable ally or even a willing dupe now that he's lost you to the Kingdom of God.

So, the battle is on. Suddenly you find yourself attacked on one level or another. The attack may come as a complete surprise—the loss of something or someone dear, ill health, or perhaps a sense of frustration in every good thing you are attempting to do.

If you give in to despair, depression or self-pity, you allow the Enemy to win with very little effort on his part.

Problems, then, are inevitable. They are part of the price we pay for living in a world which has fallen into sin.

You need to pray for special wisdom from God. You also need some keys for successful living.

In writing to the Church at Ephesus, Paul reminded his readers:

You were taught, with regard to your former way of life, to put off your old self, which is being corrupted by its deceitful desires; to be made new in the attitude of your minds; and to put on the new self, created to be like God in true righteousness and holiness (Ephesians 4:22-24).

Christians must stop living on the basis of feelings and start living on the principles of God's Word. That's what it means to be made new in the attitude of your minds. We have a new mindset, a new frame of reference—God's Word.

Second, Paul writes that Christians must "put off" or remove their old selves. In other words, we must deliberately leave our former manner of life. We must develop new habits of living.

Notice that God's advice is not negative. God demands *positive* action! We must "put off the old self," "be made new" and "put on the new self." We must actively restructure our lives so they line up with the powerful Word of God.

As President Woodrow Wilson wrote, "I am sorry for the men who do not read the Bible every day. I wonder why they deprive themselves of the strength and of the pleasure. It is one of the most singular books in the world, for every time you open it, some old text that you have read a score of times suddenly beams with a new meaning. There is no other book that I know of, of which this is true: There is no other book that yields its meaning so personally, that seems to fit itself so intimately to the very spirit that is seeking its guidance."

Problem solving is seldom easy, but without God's help it's impossible. The rest of this chapter focuses on specific problems in the light of the Bible.

FEAR

If there is one universal emotion regardless of age, it is fear.

In American culture, fear almost always is seen as a sign of weakness. We live in a macho, hero-oriented civilization which tries to con all of us into believing that fear spells weakness. *Nothing could be further from the truth!*

Fear can be a healthy emotion. Perhaps you remember touching a hot stove when you were a baby. After you felt pain from the burn, what reminded you not to touch that stove-monster again? *Fear.*

The first thing you must do, therefore, in learning to handle fear, is *recognize it as a safety emotion.* Fear keeps us from falling off cliffs or touching hot stoves. It alerts us to dangers—even dangers in human relationships.

There is no question—fear is *not* pleasant. If you've ever panicked, you know the emotion perfectly. One by-product of a terrifying situation is your fear of the situation repeating itself. If the experience produced great amounts of fear, as falling off a high place and being seriously injured, a phobia may develop.

Fear can immobolize you. As a safety emotion, fear sometimes stops you dead in your tracks. When you look over a cliff, it's good to be afraid!

No matter what you fear, God's Word points to the antidote. St. John writes, **"There is no fear in love. But perfect love drives out fear"** (I John 4:18). Only the power of love can overcome fear. The realization that love casts out fear is the key to controlling and overcoming inappropriate fear.

But, what is love? John answers that question for us: **"This is love for God, to obey his commands"** (I John 5:3). So then, if love casts out fear, then it's also true that keeping God's commandments enables us to eliminate fear. It's just that simple! You may ask, "What are the commands of God?" Every word of the Bible, the book He has given us so we may know how to love and serve Him.

Singer Debby Boone admits she has had to battle nervousness, despite her notable professional successes. "I was concerned with pleasing audiences when I should have been concerned with pleasing God," she confessed. "I still dread being nervous, but I see now how God uses this. I rely constantly on the passage in Scripture where the Lord says to the Apostle Paul, *'My strength is made perfect in weakness'* " (II Corinthians 12:9).

Finally, to overcome fear, we must be willing to say, "Let the fear come. I won't fight it. After all, it's no sin to be afraid. I'm not going to worry about the fear. I have too much to accomplish in doing the will of God to worry about that."

DEPRESSION

All of us feel "down" from time to time. St. Paul, writing to the Corinthians, noted that *"We are hard pressed on every side, but not crushed; perplexed, but not in despair; persecuted, but not abandoned; struck down, but not destroyed"* (II Corinthians 4:8,9). We may simply be having a "bad" day. Perhaps we are not physically feeling good, or a situation in our life has brought us great sadness. Whatever the reason, we all have experienced depression.

But depression is not simply that "down" feeling we sometimes get. Depression is that "out" response that accompanies the down feeling—to be depressed is to be down *and* out. Depression means we quit functioning, as a result of a down feeling—to shun our responsibilities because we don't feel good.

Depression occurs when we handle a "down" period incorrectly. We may be blue or discouraged because of a sin problem that makes us aware of our guilt; or perhaps we feel "down" because of sickness, or financial or marital hardship.

Discouragement leads to depression, when we give up. We give in to our "down feelings." We let our responsibilities and interests slide. We don't feel like doing them—we don't feel like doing our job. Instead, we brood.

While we're brooding, we know we should be doing our job—fulfilling our responsibilities—and that knowledge increases our guilt. If our depression is caused by another guilt matter, we seek to ignore *all* our guilt. We spiral down into a deep, crippling depression.

Sometimes our depression shows up in other areas. Physically, we may have trouble sleeping, experience appetite loss, weight loss, a lack of energy. Our thought patterns will be affected. We may find it hard to concentrate or remember things; we may entertain thoughts of death or suicide. We may feel irritable, fearful, gloomy, teary-eyed, critical, or we may exhibit the opposite emotions as a mask; extreme quietness, giddiness, inappropriate laughter.

Severe depression increases the risk of suicide. A sense of giving up and loss of control may be the next steps.

What must you do to combat depression? You must first of all ask God's forgiveness. It's no sin to be blue or discouraged, but to neglect your job and fail to fulfill your responsibilities is a sin. Confess your guilt to God, asking for His help in combatting the depression.

Next, make up your mind to do your job and fulfill your responsibilities regardless of how you feel. If you are physically ill, take care of yourself. But don't use your illness as an excuse to avoid work, unless you absolutely must.

Also, when you feel down or discouraged, avoid the temptation to brood or feel sorry for yourself. The time spent in brooding is time you should be spending doing your job.

One sure sign of brooding is the constant use of negative vocabulary—such as, "things are hopeless" or "I can't take it anymore." When you catch yourself falling into such a mind set, back up and reassess your situation. Recognize that you are discouraged or blue, but continue to fulfill your responsibilities.

A sign outside a small church in upstate New York sums it up pretty well: "Failure is the line of least persistence."

Finally, if you immediately straighten out any relationship to God or man that has gone sour, you will avoid most occasions for depression. Poor personal relationships cause more discouragement and disillusionment than all other reasons combined.

GRIEF

Grief is one of the most perplexing and painful problems we must learn to handle. When a lifeshaking loss occurs, we feel devastated. We don't know where to turn, and our grief overwhelms us.

Grief is not simply sorrow—it is *painful* sorrow. Although we usually think of grief in connection with the death of someone very dear to us, grief can be caused by a significant loss of any sort. Men and women grieve following divorce or the loss of a job. A period of grief often follows the loss of possessions or even the loss of status. Any significant loss can provide occasion for grief.

There are real uses for grief. It is healthy to express sorrow after a significant loss, such as the death of a close family member or particularly good friend. God created us with emotions, and we shouldn't hesitate to express them. As Jesus stood by the grave of His friend Lazarus, He so visibly wept that the Jews who observed Him exclaimed, ***"See how He loved him!"*** (John 11:36). Jesus was not wrong to sorrow greatly as a result of the death of His friend. Christ's weeping is an honest expression of the deep loss that He felt—He grieved over the death of Lazarus.

For us, grief becomes a problem only when it drifts into despair. As an overwhelming sense of desperation fills you, you feel like giving up. At this point, grief becomes a serious problem.

Joe and Helen, elderly and childless, felt shattered at the news of Helen's inoperable cancer. Grief threatened to overwhelm them at first, until they decided on a plan: they would not panic, would trust God, and would get further medical opinions.

Together they drew near to God and to one another, gained strength—day-by-day, month after long month—from the Word of God, and through prayer.

Months later, a physician shook his head in disbelief. "I don't know how to explain this," he said, "but everything is normal."

"We experienced a miracle," Joe said. "Not just a miracle of physical healing, but far beyond that—we learned first-hand the power of God's Word. We learned to deal with our own fear and grief. We learned that faith conquers fear."

Paul writes in I Thessalonians 4:13, *"Brothers we do not want you to be ignorant about those who fall asleep, or to grieve like the rest of men, who have no hope."* Paul does not say Christians may not grieve after the death of a family member or friend; rather, he says we must not grieve as those *who have not hope.* That small four-word phrase is the key to overcoming the problem of grief that moves into despair.

Hope is the anchor that keeps you from drifting into despair. The Christian has no reason to despair—to give up after a loss. A non-Christian may despair because he has no hope. He doesn't know that *"in all things God works for the good of those who love Him"* (Romans 8:28).

Christians must trust in God, regardless of their loss. Even though we may not understand *why,* we can rest assured *that* God loves us and is working out everything for our good. Without this *hope*—without this *faith* in the all-governing hand of God, all our sorrows would turn into despair.

Further, we know that when a Christian dies, he or she goes to be with the Lord in heaven. Although the death of a Christian brother or sister may be extremely painful, in the midst of our sorrow, we can experience joy.

The death of a Christian is a bittersweet moment. Though we grieve over our loss, we also have the *fact* of eternal life. Our friend may be dead to this life, but he is definitely alive in heaven with the Lord.

Grief should not be shunned. Loss can be terribly painful; if ignored, it leads to even more problems—fear, anger, resentment, worry, guilt, and bitterness. To deal with grief, one must recognize the pain, endure the sorrow, but never lose sight of the *hope* that you as a Christian have in Christ.

INFERIORITY AND INADEQUACY

How many times have you heard, "So-and-so has an *inferiority complex?*" Or maybe at one time or another you have justified your lack of confidence in yourself to do a particular job by saying, "I just don't *feel* adequate" or "I *feel* inferior."

Everyone occasionally feels inferior or inadequate. Don't be fooled into thinking you're the only one who wrestles with such issues. We all do. They're problems for everyone. The trick is knowing how to deal with them.

First, problems of inferiority and inadequacy don't

spring from the emotions. *The problem is not how you feel.* Inferiority is a judgment. When you say, "I *feel* inferior" you are really saying, "I judge myself to be inferior."

No one likes to think of himself as inferior, and, therefore, bad feelings result. Furthermore, inferiority is always related to a particular situation. We judge ourselves to be inferior for a particular task, and if left unchecked, that feeling of inferiority is transferred to the rest of our life.

We can't solve the problem by dealing with our feelings. That would be like treating a symptom and not the disease. Rather, we must deal with the judgment we are making about ourselves, "I judge myself to be inferior or inadequate."

When you find yourself feeling inferior, ask yourself, "Is this judgment sound?" In other words, is the judgment you are making about yourself a good one? Is it correct?

For instance, let's assume you just started a new job. You will be doing more challanging and rewarding work; hence, more difficult work.

After the third day on your new job, you begin to wonder if you will *ever* get the hang of it. A sinking feeling begins to develop deep in your stomach, and a sense of inferiority and inadequacy overtakes you. As you walk down the hall of your office building, you notice other people who do the same job you are hired to do. Your thoughts run like this: "They are doing a good job, so why don't I? Maybe they are smarter—or younger—or more skilled?" Finally, you decide, "I guess I'm just not cut out for this job. I might as well go back to being a nobody."

This sense of inferiority is serious. If not dealt with, it will affect many other areas of your life. What should you do?

First, realize that the problem is not a feeling, but a *judgment of inferiority.* Once you recognize that, the problem-solving process can be begun.

Next, examine the judgment. Let's assume that in the case of the new job, the judgment is incorrect. After the judgment is examined, you realize you are still in the adjustment period of your new job. You recognize that you have amply demonstrated your skills and qualifications in the past, and that there is no reason for you to feel inadequate.

After such a self-assessment has been made, the sense of inferiority will be lifted. At this point it is even common to discover a renewed vigor to tackle the tough assignment. Confidence is restored along with a refreshed outlook and a renewed purpose.

But what if you discover that the judgment is true? What if, based on the facts at hand, you discover that you really are inadequate or inferior for a particular job? What do you do then? You must first of all recognize the fact. It is no sin to be inferior. We cannot excel in everything we attempt.

What if you are inferior in something in which you ought to excel? Just accept the fact that you are inferior in a particular area, but it is an area in which you must excel—perhaps in your vocation. At that point, instead of yielding to depression, lay out a plan for achieving the skills or knowledge that you need. Refuse to feel sorry for yourself. Instead, set yourself on a course to achieving your goal.

Finally, as a Christian, recognize that inferiority and inadequacy are part of the human condition. When Adam fell into sin, sinfulness and imperfection became a part of each member of the human race. We cannot escape this basic deficiency, but we can work to correct it the best way possible.

In the case of sin, our only help is in the work of Jesus Christ. The only successful way to combat inferiority and inadequacy is through God's strength, and in our reliance upon the directions He gives us in His Word.

WORRY

Worry is a sin. There are no two ways about it. Jesus said,

> *Therefore I tell you, do not worry about your life, what you will eat or drink; or about your body, what you will wear...So do not worry, saying, "What shall we eat?" or "What shall we drink?" or "What shall we wear?" For the pagans run after all these things, and your heavenly Father knows that you need them. But seek first his kingdom and his righteousness, and all these things will be given to you as well. Therefore do not worry about tomorrow, for tomorrow will worry about itself. Each day has enough trouble of its own* (Matthew 6:25-34).

Worry obviously isn't good for us. In fact, the Bible even says it's a sin.

But, *because* worry is a sin, there is hope! We have seen elsewhere in this book that Jesus came to die for and deal with sin. Worry can, therefore, be overcome! Through the power of the Holy Spirit whose instructions are found in the Bible, we can achieve victory over worry.

As you may have guessed, worry is the sinful perversion of a good emotion—concern. As such, we cannot simply turn our "worry" off. We must learn to replace worry with the proper emotion—concern. But how do we do that?

Concern becomes worry when it is focused upon the wrong day—*tomorrow* (Matthew 6:34). Because tomorrow is not yet here, the energy and anxiety created by our worry cannot be properly channeled—they cannot be released.

As Jesus said, *"We could worry from now until the day we die about the length of our life, but we will nevertheless not add one hour to it"* (Matthew 6:27). It is futile to worry. It accomplishes little beyond tired, dissatisfied feelings or perhaps, eventually, an ulcer!

Worry can be overcome only by refocusing our concern

upon today's tasks (Matthew 6:34). Concerned about *today's* problems, we channel our resources productively, to solve each problem. That may make us feel tired at the end of the day, but satisfied, also!

Instead of having a nagging worry plague you all night, feelings of satisfaction will enter your sleep. Your concern for the present has borne fruit with the accomplishments of your day. Hence, satisfaction results.

Worry, or that diffused cloud of fear we know as anxiety, can become so habitual that we scarcely recognize that we're indulging ourselves. One grandmother found a sure cure for her worry habit: "I give myself three minutes by the kitchen timer," she said. "Then I make myself stop. I say, 'Lord, my three minutes are up. You take it from here!' And I assume He does!"

How can you eliminate worry? The first thing you must do is make plans for tomorrow. God plans (Ephesians 1:3-6), and you should too.

Secondly, submit your plans to God and leave the outcome entirely to Him. Attempt to do what you planned, but if God allows something to intervene—so be it. Don't worry. You did what you should. Accept the obstacle as coming from His hand and see what can be learned from it.

For example, let's suppose you have just purchased a piece of property. You and your family decide to build a house there. You choose a home site and you are ready to build. There's just one problem. A road must be cleared through the trees, to bring in materials from which to build the house.

You determine that you have ten days to chop down the trees. Unless the builder begins to build the house in ten days he won't be able to finish before winter. You assemble your equipment and begin to chop down trees. On the morning

LIFE'S PROBLEMS

... "Therefore I tell you,
do not worry about your life,
what you will eat;
or about your body,
what you will wear...

Consider how the lilies grow.
They do not labor or spin.
Yet I tell you,
not even Solomon in all his splendor
was dressed like one of these.
If that is how God clothes the grass
of the field, which is here today,
and tomorrow is thrown into the fire,
how much more will he clothe you,
O you of little faith!
Luke 12: 23, 23 and 27, 28

of the fifth day, it begins to thunder. Lightning follows, with very heavy rains. Because of the weather, you have to quit work. Not only does the storm keep you from working the fifth day, but the sixth also. You are now two days behind! There is no way you will finish the job in ten days!

Does it do any good to worry? Of course not. All that you can do is accept the delay as from the hand of God. He knows you need to finish building your house before the winter. He won't make you and your family sleep in the snow! Perhaps He'll postpone winter for a couple of days! Whatever He decides to do, have faith that God will take care of you.

GUILT

Guilt is a universal problem, because all men are sinners (Romans 3:23). Because of that, the first way we properly deal with guilt is to *acknowledge it.*

Guilt is not an emotion. In biblical terms, guilt is a position before God. All men stand before God guilty or not guilty. If we are Christians, the blood of Jesus Christ has cleansed us from all sin. We have been declared *not guilty* before God.

But does that mean we never break God's commands? Or does it mean that we always do what God requires? Obviously not. We continue to sin as long as we live. Because we do, we must deal with guilt.

To deal properly with guilt, we recognize that we have sinned—first against God, secondarily against others. We are not just sick and in need of healing, nor are we simply alienated, in need of a restored fellowship. We are sinners and guilty before God. We need forgiveness—even as Christians.

The busy housewife yells at Todd, her five-year-old,

whacks him across the rear of his muddy jeans and calls him a bad boy. The "crime"? He'd waded in the stream he was forbidden to visit, then tracked through her freshly waxed kitchen.

"Go to your room without lunch!" she commands.

Crestfallen, the little guy turns a pleading look in her direction. "Okay, mommy," comes the sad reply. "I can do without lunch, I guess. But are you ever going to love me any more?"

Mother and son both need forgiveness. God's Word teaches how to forgive. It says much about the enormous power forgiveness releases into all relationships.

Also, we can blame no one but ourselves. We must be willing to say, "*I* have done wrong; it is no one's fault but my own. It is not the fault of my parents, my spouse, my church, society, school, or God. It is *my* fault. *I* am guilty."

Finally, we must confess our sin to God. John writes, *"If we claim to be without sin, we deceive ourselves and the truth is not in us. If we confess our sins, he is faithful and just and will forgive us our sins and purify us from all unrighteouness"* (I John 1:8,9). We must seek God's forgiveness confessing our sins. Further, if we have offended anyone else, we also must ask His forgiveness.

There's a second type of guilt that creates problems for Christians today. It is a false guilt.

We pointed out earlier that guilt is a position before God. We also saw that a man is guilty on the basis of his actions — what he *does.* If we do what God says in His Word, we are not guilty. If we fail to do what He says, we are guilty. It's that simple.

False guilt, therefore, is feeling guilty about something that is perfectly acceptable to God.

For instance, someone tells you that you must give fifty

Therefore, as God's chosen people,
holy and dearly loved, clothe youselves
with compassion, kindness, humility,
gentleness and patience. Bear with each
other and forgive whatever grievances
you may have against one another.
Forgive as the Lord forgave you.
Colossians 3:12,13

percent of everything you earn to God. He says, "If you *really* love God, you will give Him 50%." You know you give God only ten percent of your income. You immediately feel guilty, thinking you haven't done what God requires. You think, "I guess I don't *really* love God as much as I thought."

How do you handle this guilt? First, go to the Bible and make sure your actions are really wrong. In this case, you discover that God requires only ten percent. He says, if you give ten percent of your income to Him, He will bless you, opening up the windows of heaven (Malachi 3:10).

However, if you *are* doing wrong—if you are indeed sinning—follow the steps outlined above and elsewhere in this book.

People today may try to lay a "guilt trip" on you. Don't be fooled. The only thing you should feel guilty about is sin—sin as defined in the Bible. Anything else, don't worry!

ANGER

In spite of what many of us were taught in the past, anger is not *always* wrong. For example, God is angry with the wicked. The expression of that anger is His destruction of them. Anger, then, is an emotion which mobilizes the necessary force to destroy something. God is angry with the wicked, and He ultimately will destroy them.

Anger in this sense is not wrong. It is a good thing to be angry with evil and wickedness. The problem arises when anger is expressed in a wrong way, when force is mobilized to express anger through unbiblical or sinful action. Paul refers to this when he writes, *"In your anger, do not sin"* (Ephesians 4:26).

When is anger sinful, and therefore a problem? The first instance is, when anger is born from selfishness. Too often we get angry over the most insignificant things. If someone doesn't do a thing *exactly* as we want, or if they don't treat us *exactly* as we feel we should be treated, we become angry.

Any time you become angry for a selfish reason—when anger springs from pride, hurt feelings, and the like, you may be sure the anger is wrong and will cause problems. Be quick to *put it off! "In your anger, do not sin"* (Ephesians 4:26).

A young wife wrote about her husband's habit of taking long hunting trips, leaving her at home with three young children. "My silent anger towards him mounted and mounted. Though Bill was a good husband and father, I began to look for reasons to justify my anger towards him, and hunt other flaws I could criticize.

"My anger led to a break down in communications. Bill grew more distant because he knew every time we spoke I would criticize him. It was best that we didn't speak at all. Anger over my husband's hunting trips contaminated every aspect of our marriage.

"Eventually our pastor had to set me straight. Anger over one selfish complaint—his hunting trips—almost led me into the sin of divorce! Instead of allowing the anger I felt to tear me apart from the inside out, I went to Bill and told him how I felt. Instead of criticizing, I tried to understand. The lines of communication were established once again."

Anger is sinful whenever it is expressed in wrong actions. An obvious example is when we "blow up" at someone. Psychologists sometimes call this "ventilating." God calls it sin.

Instead of using the energy mobilized by our anger to tear up evil, *when we blow up, we tear up others.* Solomon wrote, *"A fool gives full vent to his anger"* (Proverbs 29:11). Even when you have "good reason" to be angry, why waste all that energy blowing up and tearing someone up? Far better to be the *"wise man"* and *"keep yourself under control"* (Proverbs 29:11).

Do not hate your brother
in your heart.
Rebuke your neighbor frankly
so you will not share
in his guilt.
Do not seek revenge
or bear a grudge
against one of your people,
but love your neighbor
as yourself.
I am the Lord.
Leviticus 19:17-18

Use the energy to destroy evil and sin in your life rather than hurting someone else. It is never right to "blow up" in anger.

You may say, "I *never* blow up. Even when I am angry, I am always in control." Are you *really* always in control? Maybe you don't blow up, but perhaps you express your anger in another way. Some people don't blow up, but they do *clam up.* And that is equally wrong.

Moses writes in Leviticus 19:17-18, *"Do not hate your brother in your heart. Rebuke your neighbor frankly so you will not share in his guilt. Do not seek revenge or bear a grudge against one of your people, but love your neighbor as yourself. I am the LORD."* Why does God say to rebuke your neighbor and not to hold a grudge in the same sentence that he commands us to love our neighbors as ourselves?

What happens to you when a close friend does something wrong to you? You become angry, but then you clam up without confronting the friend with his wrong. Very likely, your stomach becomes tied in knots. Every time the incident comes to your mind your anger is rekindled, and the whole ugly scene continues. When you clam up, whom do you hurt? No one but yourself. Your energy is wasted by tearing up yourself.

Well, if we're not to blow up *or* clam up, how should we express our anger?

In fact, what is the biblical principle for dealing with anger? Ephesians 4:26 reads, *"Do not let the sun go down while you are still angry."* In other words, your anger should be dealt with immediately. If the anger itself is sinful—if it grows out of selfishness—you must recognize it and immediately put it off. If, however, your reason for anger is righteous, what should you do?

We know we must neither blow up *or* clam up. We must act as the wise man in Proverbs, and release the energy of our anger while under control. We must not tear up others or ourselves. Rather, we must aim at tearing up the *problem,* and where necessary, build up other people.

Where possible, gently confront the person who has angered you, pointing out the unrighteousness of his or her actions. Take the advice of the Apostle Paul seriously, ***"Do not let unwholesome talk come out of your mouths, but only what is helpful for building others up according to their needs, that it may benefit those who listen"*** (Ephesians 4:29). That's *power for living!*

By now you sense something of the tremendous adventure the Christian life offers to all who want thrilling new dimensions in powerful living.

Adventure, of course, requires a daring willingness to grow. As you eagerly and expectantly begin your new walk with Jesus Christ, look to His Word for perfect signposts toward growth.

You'll want to begin growing. You desire more *power for living!*

But from everlasting to everlasting
the Lord's love is with those
who fear him,
and his righteousness with their
children's children —
with those who keep his covenant
and remember to obey his precepts.
Psalm 103: 17, 18

HOW TO
KEEP ON
GROWING

Becoming a Christian is not the end of the road! Instead, it's the first step on a wonderful new path. God rarely takes people to heaven the moment they become Christians. He has work for them here.

This is God's world. Even though sin has polluted it, God has not abandoned His world. He plans to be glorified through His creation.

That's where Christians come in. They are God's *"new creation"* (II Corinthians 5:17), living examples of what God plans to do throughout the universe someday when He makes a *complete "new creation"—"a new heaven and a new earth"* (Revelation 21:1). That makes Christians a sort of "preview of coming attractions." *"We are therefore Christ's ambassadors, as though God were making his appeal through us. We implore you on God's behalf: be reconciled to God"* (II Corinthians 5:20).

You are Christ's personal ambassador to the world. Sounds like a tall order, doesn't it? How can you possibly accomplish such a commission?

In **POWER FOR LIVING,** you'll learn what God says you need in order to be effectively prepared for this task. One word sums it up: *maturity.* There's another word for it: *growth.*

The basic ingredients of growth are outlined in this acrostic:

G Go to God in prayer daily (John 15:7).

R Read God's Word daily (Acts 17:11) — begin with the Gospel of John.

O Obey God, moment by moment (John 14:21).

W Witness for Christ by your life and words (Matthew 4:19; John 15:8).

T Trust God for every detail of your life (IPeter 5:7).

H Holy Spirit — allow Him to control and empower your daily life and witness (Galatians 5:16,17; Acts 1:8).

G
GO TO GOD IN PRAYER DAILY

Prayer is our most basic expression of a living faith in God: it is the "breathing" of our spiritual life, through which we communicate with Him. Actually, it's as simple as talking with God.

Prayer doesn't have to be long, or formal, or phrased in technical language. A short, sincere expression of thanks — or a cry for help — reaches God's ear as surely as any flowery petition delivered in a great cathedral or the halls of Congress. God loves us. He wants us to come to Him regularly in conversational prayer.

Conversational prayer. "Forgive me, Father. I guess it must be as tough to be a teenage girl as it is to be the *mother* of a teenage girl. Give me patience instead of nagging."

—"Lord, this is the day to end all days. We're buying our house! You provided...You said You would...and now it's ours...Thank You, thank You!"

—"Dear God, if I can't balance my checkbook, how can I figure this income tax return? Help!"

— "Father, I've got a station wagon full of five-year-olds. It's a good thing You go along on carpools."

— "Jesus, thank You that I'm not scared of the dark."

— "Lord, you said you care about every detail of our lives. Now about that extra ten pounds I'm carrying around . . ."

Take note of the especially youthful, energetic and joyous Christians you meet. Almost certainly, they know a secret: *prayer provides power for living.*

Will God Answer "Yes" or "No"

Consider God's attitude toward prayer. Jesus told the story about a poor widow who had been treated unjustly (Luke 18:1-8). She took her case to a judge who, Jesus said, *"neither feared God nor cared about men."* He refused to listen to her, but she didn't give up asking. She kept returning with the same old request. The woman pestered the judge so much he finally said to himself, *"Even though I don't fear God or care about men, yet because this woman keeps bothering me, I will see that she gets justice, so that she won't eventually wear me out with her coming!"*

The Bible says Jesus told his disciples this story *"to show them that they should always pray and not give up."* Now, Jesus didn't mean that God is like that unfair old judge. God is a loving Father to us. The point is, if even an unfair judge will listen to someone who keeps coming to him, how much *more* will God listen to His children!

Another time, Jesus put it this way: *"Which of you, if his son asks for bread, will give him a stone? Or if he asks for a fish, will give him a snake? If you then, though you are evil, know how to give good gifts to your children, how much more will your Father in heaven give good gifts to those who ask him!"* (Matthew 7:9-11).

God *wants* to grant our requests, much more than the most loving father on earth wishes to give his children good things. Imagine a father who is rich enough to afford every imaginable gift, who loves his children and wants them to be happy—and who *enjoys* giving them good gifts! Would such a father refuse any reasonable request?

Of course, every parent knows that a child will sometimes ask for something harmful; sometimes, a child isn't mature enough to handle what he wants to have. Earthly parents have to say "No" for these reasons. Sometimes God says "No" to us for similar reasons.

It's important to remember this: When God says "No" to us, it's *not* because He can't afford it. God owns everything! And, when He says "No," it's *not* because He doesn't care about us, or because He isn't interested in our problems. God loves us more than any earthly father ever could. Although God *can* and *does* say "No" it is *unusual* for Him to do so. *God's usual response to His children's prayers is "Yes!"*

We should pray *expecting* a "Yes" answer. The Bible says when we don't have what we need, often it's simply because we don't *ask* (James 4:2).

A businessman decided to keep complete records of the prayers he prayed and answers received. "I quit after a month" he confessed. "I saw God was answering so fast that I found myself keeping records instead of praying more prayers!"

"Write down your prayers, if you want to become convinced that God absolutely *does* answer them!"

Do you have needs? (Of course!) Why not make a list of them today and read the list as you pray to your Father in heaven? But remember the story Jesus told about the widow and the judge—*keep asking!*

A Few Rules to Remember

God has given us some principles about prayer to keep in mind. The first one, *we must be Christians.* Jesus said, ***"I am the way and the truth and the life. No one comes to the Father except through me"*** (John 14:6). Are you a Christian?

God wants you to get the *most important* prayer out of the way first, before you come to Him with other problems. Just think: what if God gave you everything you asked for, *without* first saving you from your sins? Wouldn't that be a disaster? You'd think you didn't need a thing! You'd feel as if you had it made—while all the time, you'd be lost.

Christians usually end their prayers with these words: *In Jesus' Name* (see John 16:23). That isn't just a handy little phrase. It expresses the very foundation of our right to come before God with our requests. We aren't coming in our own name. We are allowed to come to God *only* because *Jesus Christ exchanged places with us* (II Corinthians 5:21). He was punished for our sins, and *we* get treated by God as if we had lived a perfect life! Our access to God is "in Jesus' name."

God tells us, first, to come to Him for salvation. If you are not yet a Christian, turn back a few pages—right now—to the section on "How to Get Right With God" and pay close attention to its message. The most important prayer you'll ever pray is that which provides the basis for everything else: turning to Jesus Christ and receiving Him as your Saviour. This is where prayer must begin.

Second, *we must be obedient Christians.* Jesus said, ***"If you remain in me and my words remain in you, ask whatever you wish, and it will be given you"*** (John 15:7). A songwriter in the Bible put it this way: ***"If I had cherished sin in my heart, the Lord would not have listened; but God has surely listened and heard my voice in prayer. Praise be to***

God, who has not rejected my prayer or withheld his love from me!" (Psalm 66:18-20; see also Proverbs 28:9).

Third, *we must pray according to God's will. "This is the assurance we have in approaching God: that if we ask anything according to his will, he hears us. And if we know that he hears us— whatever we ask— we know that we have what we asked of him"* (I John 5:14,15).

But this seems to raise a problem: how can we know God's will? Do we have to be able to look into the future to see what He wants to do? No, of course not. Actually, it's pretty easy to know God's will, in the sense meant by the verse quoted above. God has authored the Bible *to tell us exactly what His will is.*

Obviously, God hasn't told us in detail everything He plans for every moment of our future. He has His "secrets," so to speak. But He *has* told us His will for our lives (how He wants us to live). He *has* told us what to pray for, and what He will answer: *"The secret things belong to the LORD our God, but the things revealed belong to us and to our children forever, that we may follow all the words of this law"* (Deuteronomy 29:29).

You will find *thousands* of promises in the Bible about *specific ways in which God answers prayer.* Take these promises personally. Ask God to answer you on the basis of what He Himself has said. Then realize that these promises are simply the bare outline of what God can do— because the Bible says that God can do *"immeasurably more than all we ask or imagine"* (Ephesians 3:20). God can do far more than you think He can!

A Pattern for Prayer

Many Christians pray what is commonly called *The Lord's Prayer* (Matthew 6:9-13) as a regular part of both personal worship and worship in church. You may recall it from childhood.

But Jesus also gave this prayer to his followers as a *pattern* or *model* for prayer. We may repeat it as a prayer in itself, but we should also see it as a pattern, containing the "basic ingredients"of good, effective, and powerful praying. Here, then, is the six-step outline from *The Lord's Prayer:*

1. *Our Father in heaven, hallowed be your name*—Pray that God will be hallowed *(honored)* by all people everywhere (Matthew 5:16).

2. *Your kingdom come*—Pray that God's kingly rule will come, so that every knee will bow before Jesus Christ (Philippians 2:10-11).

3. *Your will be done on earth as it is in heaven*—Pray that people on earth will obey God's will, just as the angels do (Psalm 103: 20, 21; Micah 6:8).

4. *Give us today our daily bread*—Pray that God will supply what you need, and will also enable you to enjoy the many good gifts in His world (Philippians 4:6, 19).

5. *Forgive us our debts, as we also have forgiven our debtors*—Pray that God will pardon your sins against Him, just as He makes you able to forgive what others have done against you (Matthew 6:14-15).

6. *And lead us not into temptation, but deliver us from the evil one*—Pray that God will protect you from tempting situations, and that He will support you when you are tempted, so that you will be strong enough to come through trials successfully (I Corinthians 10:13).

Just think what this means. God has *promised* to answer our prayers, if they are according to His will. And here, He has provided us with a perfect example of what He wants us to ask. What could be better? If we pray faithfully in this way, God has *promised* that He will say *Yes!*

Learn to pray. Don't keep your problems to yourself.

Don't just complain to other people. Take your problems to God, who listens and answers. *"Cast all your anxiety on him because he cares for you"* (I Peter 5:7).

R
READ GOD'S WORD DAILY

The importance of a regular reading of God's Word cannot be overestimated. This is because *the Bible is absolutely central to our lives.* There are several reasons for this.

First, *the Bible, by the power of God's Spirit, produces faith in our hearts.* By hearing God's Word, we are spiritually "reborn" into God's Kingdom: *"He chose to give us birth through the word of truth"* (James 1:18). *"For you have been born again, not of perishable seed, but of imperishable, through the living and enduring word of God"* (I Peter 1:23). Our Christian life begins with the Word of God.

Second, *the Bible continues to nourish us throughout our lives.* Jesus Himself prayed that the Bible would have this effect upon His followers: *"Sanctify them by the truth; your word is truth"* (John 17:17). *(Sanctify means set apart and make holy.)*

How does God make us holy? By bringing us into regular contact with His Word. Our growth in the Christian life is dependent upon our feeding on the Bible and its truths. Speaking of the Bible, the Apostle Peter wrote: *"Like newborn babies, crave pure spiritual milk, so that by it you may grow up in your salvation"* (I Peter 2:2; see also II Peter 3:18).

Third, *the Bible is our standard for making decisions and forming opinions in every area of life.* *"All Scripture is God-breathed and is useful for teaching, rebuking, correcting and training in righteousness, so that the man of God may be thoroughly equipped for every good work"* (II Timothy

3:16,17). Every moment of our lives, we are forced to make judgments—at home, on the job, in school, regarding our friendships, and so on. But we are not on our own. God has given us a standard for all of life that is *absolute.*

A salesman tells about advice he heard at a men's prayer breakfast: "Men, study the Book of Proverbs for guidance in business. It's the best book of business principles ever written."

The salesman learned there are thirty-one chapters in that Book, (one for each day of the month) and decided to read one each morning at the beginning of his business day. "I began that very day on Chapter Three," he related, "and came to a verse that said not to withhold money you owe, when you were able to repay it (Proverbs 3:27-28).

"I thought of a note I had at the bank. I didn't need to pay it yet, but I did have the money. I decided to repay it that day.

"Two years later, my banker reminded me of that episode. He was so impressed that I took the Scriptures at their word that he decided then and there he'd always be willing to work with me on future ventures. Obeying God helped my credit rating."

Why was the Bible written? It wasn't intended just for church services. *The Bible is God's Word for all of life.* It was written *"for attaining wisdom and discipline; for understanding words of insight; for acquiring a disciplined and prudent life, doing what is right and just and fair"* (Proverbs 1:2,3). The Creator of the world has given us a "User's Manual" to explain how it works! Success, in every area of life, comes from *understanding* and *applying* the Bible, the Word of God (Joshua 1:8; Psalm 1:1-3).

So we should get into the habit of reading the Bible on a daily basis. We must go on a "treasure hunt" for God's wisdom in Holy Scripture, with the attitude that it is indeed a storehouse of fabulous wealth: *"If you look for it as silver and search for it as for hidden treasure, then you will understand the fear of the LORD and find the knowledge of God. For the LORD gives wisdom, and from his mouth comes knowledge and understanding"* (Proverbs 2:4-6).

We can make all kinds of mistakes as we go through life. An understanding of the Bible's practical wisdom, however, will keep us from falling into disaster. A solid knowledge of the Bible's standards and priorities can keep us safe from the kind of destructive and life-ruining choices people around us are making every day. *"Then you will understand what is right and just and fair — every good path. For wisdom will enter your heart, and knowledge will be pleasant to your soul. Discretion will protect you, and understanding will guard you"* (Proverbs 2:9-11).

O

OBEY GOD, MOMENT BY MOMENT

Do you love Jesus Christ? Could you prove it if you had to? One of the most exciting things in the world is that God has given us a *standard* for love. We all know that there are all kinds of phony counterfeits of "love" in the world. A lot of bad and even cruel things have been done in the name of "love."

So, what is God's standard? Jesus told us: *"Whosoever has my commands and obeys them, he is the one who loves me. He who loves me will be loved by my Father, and I too will love him and show myself to him"* (John 14:21).

All Scripture is
God-breathed
and is useful for teaching,
rebuking, correcting and training
in righteousness,
so that the man of God
may be thoroughly equipped
for every good work.
2 Timothy 3:16,17

What is the proof of our love for Jesus? *Obedience to His commands.* Of course, we don't have to "prove" anything to anybody. The point really is that the natural *result* of knowing and loving God is that we obey Him. And that's how we know we're on track—we can gauge ourselves spiritually by looking at our behavior. *"And this is love: that we walk in obedience to his commands"* (II John 6).

It isn't possible to love God apart from our relationships with others. God doesn't ask us to love Him by cutting ourselves off from everyone else, for *"he has given us this command: Whoever loves God must also love his brother"* (I John 4:21).

But how can I be sure I am loving my brother, my fellow Christian? *"This is how we know that we love the children of God: by loving God and carrying out His commands. This is love for God: to obey his commands. And his commands are not burdensome"* (I John 5:2,3).

The Apostle Paul gave *the Bible's definition of love:* *"Love is the fulfillment of the law"* (Romans 13:10). In fact, that's exactly what Jesus told some people who asked Him about the commandments. Jesus quoted from the Old Testament Law and said:

> *"Love the Lord your God with all your heart and with all your soul and with all your mind." This is the first and greatest commandment. And the second is like it: "Love your neighbor as yourself." All the Law and the Prophets hang on these two commandments* (Matthew 22:37-40; see Deuteronomy 6:5 and Leviticus 19:18).

Some people became very angry with Jesus when He spoke this way. They didn't want to obey God. They just wanted to keep their old traditions—even when their traditions were completely against God's Word! And Jesus challenged them: *"Why do you break the command of God for*

.

the sake of your tradition?" (Matthew 15:3). God's Word must always come first.

But this might seem to raise a problem. We know we are not saved by our works of obedience. In fact, only Jesus Christ has obeyed God perfectly, and He did that in our place, as our substitute.

What is the place of "good works" in the Christian's life? The Apostle Paul explained: *"For it is by grace you have been saved, through faith—and this not from yourselves, it is the gift of God—not by works, so that no one can boast"* (Ephesians 2:8,9). No question about it, we are saved through faith, not on the basis of good deeds. But then Paul said this: *"For we are God's workmanship, created in Christ Jesus to do good works, which God prepared in advance for us to do"* (Ephesians 2:10).

Of what does the Christian life consist? Doing good works, in obedience to God's commands. Our motivation for obedience is not our fear of God, but our love for Him. We are God's children, choosing to obey our loving Father in heaven. That's power for living!

The Bible says that as we grow in the faith, we get better at it. Even at the beginning, it isn't really all that hard to obey. Remember what we read earlier: *"his commands are not burdensome"* (I John 5:3). Of course, in this life we can never obey God *perfectly,* and *"if we claim to be without sin, we deceive ourselves and the truth is not in us"* (I John 1:8).

The fact remains, we can experience real and immediate growth as Christians. As we study God's Word and *internalize* its principles, obedience becomes more and more natural and spontaneous. Growth in our physical lives doesn't take concentration on our part. Growth is simply a natural result of doing such things as eating properly, exercising, and resting. In the same way, Christian growth results

Train a child in the way
he should go,
and when he is old he
will not turn from it.
Proverbs 22:6

from studying God's Word and applying it in our lives.

Spiritual growth does not merely happen to us as individuals. When we become Christians, we become members of what is called "the Body of Christ"—the people of God, the church. The Bible teaches that we grow not only as individuals, but also as *members* of the Body of Christ.

The entire Body grows together,

> *until we all reach unity in the faith and in the knowledge of the Son of God and become mature, attaining to the whole measure of the fullness of Christ. Then we will no longer be infants.... Instead, speaking the truth in love, we will in all things grow up into him who is the Head, that is, Christ. From him the whole body, joined and held together by every supporting ligament, grows and builds itself up in love, as each part does its work* (Ephesians 4:13-16).

This is why the Bible tells us to have good relationships with other Christians as an important part of our obedience. Christians help one another to obey.

> *Let us hold unswervingly to the hope we profess, for he who promised is faithful. And let us consider how we may spur one another on toward love and good deeds. Let us not give up meeting together, as some are in the habit of doing, but let us encourage one another* (Hebrews 10:23-25).

These reasons show why church membership becomes essential to healthy growth in Christ.

"I'm sixty years old and have been a 'loner' all my life" a career woman said. "Then I found the most amazing church. We appreciate one another. In ten years I have seen nothing but love, encouragement, and kindness. Nobody criticizes. Everybody helps.

"I know none of us is perfect, but I'm convinced we *can* live together in love. Where has this church been all my life?"

As you study God's Word, you discover more ways to obey God, as well as more ways to apply what you know. The possibilities of applying God's Word to the world are every bit as vast as the world itself. That's because it's God's world.

As you grow in your Christian life, remember these simple, yet profound, words of Jesus: *"If you love me, you will obey what I command"* (John 14:15).

W

WITNESS FOR CHRIST BY YOUR LIFE AND WORDS

A further aspect of our growth in Christ is our witnessing. Don't let this subject frighten you. It doesn't mean everyone must get up on a platform and preach, or pass out literature in a park. Its basic meaning is much simpler—and more total—than that.

First, God wants you to *witness through your life.* This means your personal life, your words and actions, are to reflect the character of God. Without hearing even so much as a word from you, people should know you are a Christian.

How do you accomplish that? By doing what we've been studying: obeying God's Word in every area of your life. Wherever you are—at home, work, school, or play—others should see your life lived according to God's standards.

This doesn't require you to become a prude, wear strange clothes, and be unable to have a good time. It doesn't mean you must carry a Bible around all day, either. It simply

*I tell you the truth,
unless a kernal of wheat
falls to the ground and dies,
it remains only a single seed.
But if it dies, it produces many seeds.
The man who loves his life
will lose it, while the man
who hates his life in the world
will keep it for eternal life.*
John 12:24, 25

means you take your standards for your thoughts and actions from the Word of God, rather than from those around you.

Jesus said, *"This is to my Father's glory, that you bear much fruit, showing yourselves to be my disciples.... You did not choose me, but I chose you to go and bear fruit— fruit that will last"* (John 15:8, 16). The picture Christ draws shows us as branches on a vine; He has placed us there for the specific purpose of bearing fruit. In this way, people will see we indeed belong to Christ. Our *life* is to be a testimony to people around us.

A Christian nurse in a psychiatric clinic had several opportunities to speak of her faith to doctors in the clinic. They talked among themselves about their nurse's "irrational belief system" but didn't verbally object, since she was an excellent employee.

Then the woman's much-beloved teenage son was killed in a motorcycle accident. In the weeks that followed, one physician after another approached the nurse privately, to question her about her faith. Her calm demeanor and peaceful spirit in the face of deep grief "preached a silent sermon" each finally was able to hear.

In fact, Christians are supposed to affect the whole world by their godly lifestyle, as Jesus declared:

> *You are the light of the world. A city on a hill cannot be hidden. Neither do people light a lamp and put it under a bowl. Instead they put it on its stand, and it gives light to everyone in the house. In the same way, let your light shine before men, that they may see your good deeds and praise your Father in heaven* (Matthew 5:14-16).

Get out there and let your light shine!

Second, however, God wants you to *witness by your words.* It isn't enough simply to live the right kind of life without testifying about Jesus with your mouth. The Bible commands: *"Always be prepared to give an answer to everyone who asks you to give the reason for the hope that you have"* (I Peter 3:15).

Think about this. The Bible assumes the testimony of your life will shine as the sort of example that draws people to you, asking you to witness to them! And at that point— even if you aren't a dynamic preacher or a brilliant theologian—*you have to have an answer.*

The best thing to do is to *study the New Testament.* Get a basic outline in your mind (such as "How to Get Right With God" found in Chapter III) and become familiar with how the Bible develops the salvation theme. Get to know your Bible well, so you can find your way around the Books of John and Romans, to begin with, and eventually the rest of the Bible.

While the basic message is forever the same, the way it meets people and their needs is refreshingly different. Get to know what the Bible says about those needs. Find out what the Bible says on the many issues of life. Seek to develop a *worldview*—a basic Christian *outlook* and *perspective,* so that no matter what problems come up, you will at least have a handle on the basic issues (even if you can't answer all the details).

Let's review these essentials. First, an outline of the gospel. Second, a working knowledge of the Bible. Third, a grip on what the Bible says about the issues and problems of life. And, fourth, a basic understanding of the Christian focus on what the world and life are all about. You should be deepening your knowledge of these all the time. These elements offer *power for living!*

Now, let's suppose you have a basic grasp of these points. And let's also suppose you have opportunities to talk to the following individuals: your paperboy, a fellow worker, a

*But you are a chosen people,
a royal priesthood, a holy nation,
a people belonging to God,
that you may declare praises
of him who called you out of darkness
into his wonderful light...
always be prepared to give an answer
to everyone who asks you
to give the reason
for the hope that you have.*
1 Peter 2:9 and 3:15

family member, a drug addict, a successful businessman, a pregnant teenager, a happy-go-lucky college student, a *serious* college student, a lonely and frightened immigrant, a professional philosopher, and a divorced, working mother of three children. Could you handle it?

It might not be easy. Each would require a special kind of sensitivity and wisdom. *But you could do it.* Why? Not because you're so smart. Not because you can think up a lot of snappy answers on the spot. *But because you know the Lord and are beginning to know His Book* and experience its power in your life.

Do you know what Jesus told His disciples? He said, *"Come, follow me, and I will make you fishers of men"* (Matthew 4:19). Now you have followed Him too; and by His power, you will become a "fisher of men" bringing people into His kingdom.

T

TRUST GOD FOR EVERY DETAIL OF YOUR LIFE

When God placed you into His family, He took responsibility for your life and your problems. One of the most well-loved passages in the Bible is the 23rd Psalm, which begins with these words: *"The Lord is my shepherd, I shall lack nothing"* (Psalm 23:1). God has promised to care for us, just as a loving shepherd cares for his sheep. Jesus said, *"My sheep listen to my voice; I know them, and they follow me. I give them eternal life, and they shall never perish; no one can snatch them out of my hand"* (John 10:27, 28).

God's deep concern for us meant that the Apostle Paul was able to state an absolute guarantee: *"And we know that in all things God works for the good of those who love Him, who have been called according to His purpose"* (Romans 8:28). Think about that! God is working in all things—not just the good things or the happy things, but in *all things*—for *your* good! So the Apostle Peter encouraged his readers: *"Cast all your anxiety on Him because He cares for you"* (I Peter 5:7). You can commit *every* detail of your life to the will of God, knowing that He loves you, and that His way is always best.

"Trust in the Lord with all your heart, and lean not on your own understanding. In all your ways acknowledge Him, and He will make your paths straight" (Proverbs 3:5,6). As this verse says, God positively blesses us, in every area, as we submit to Him and lean on His wisdom. Look at these other promises:

> *Trust in the LORD and do good; dwell in the land and enjoy safe pasture.*
>
> *Delight yourself in the LORD and He will give you the desires of your heart.*
>
> *Commit your way to the LORD; trust in Him and He will do this: He will make your righteousness shine like the dawn, the justice of your cause like the noonday sun* (Psalm 37:3-6).

With this great, all-powerful, loving God watching over you, do you have to be worried about your life? Do you need to be upset about what evil men might be doing? The Bible says, *Be patient! Those who trust God are going to win!*

> *Be still before the LORD and wait patiently for him; do not fret when men succeed in their ways, when they carry out their wicked schemes. Refrain from anger and turn from wrath; do not fret—it leads only to evil. For evil men will be cut off, but those who hope in the Lord will inherit the land. A little while, and the wicked will be no more; though you look for them, they will not be found. But the meek will inherit the land and enjoy great peace* (Psalm 37:7-11).

As a Christian, you can be free from worry and anxiety, because *the Christian's God is absolutely dependable.* *"Therefore, my dear brothers, stand firm. Let nothing move you. Always give yourselves fully to the work of the Lord, because you know that your labor for the Lord is not in vain"* (I Corinthians 15:58).

H

HOLY SPIRIT— ALLOW HIM TO CONTROL AND EMPOWER YOUR DAILY LIFE AND WITNESS

After Jesus ascended into heaven, He sent the Holy Spirit to come upon His disciples (see Acts 2). God's people, the church, had now become His holy temple, filled and empowered by God Himself. The Apostle Paul wrote to a Christian church: *"Don't you know that you yourselves are God's temple and that God's Spirit lives in you? If anyone destroys God's temple, God will destroy him; for God's temple is sacred, and you are that temple"* (I Corinthians 3:16, 17; see also Ephesians 2:19-22).

This means that every Christian has the responsibility to *"be filled with the Spirit"* (Ephesians 5:18). This basically means to be under the control of the Holy Spirit, living in accordance with what He wants. *"The sinful mind is hostile to God. It does not submit to God's law.... You, however, are controlled not by your sinful nature but by the Spirit, if the Spirit of God lives in you. And if anyone does not have the Spirit of Christ, he does not belong to Christ"* (Romans 8:7,9).

The powerful work of the Holy Spirit in our lives produces attitudes and actions in accordance with the Spirit's desires, as He has revealed them in the commandments: *"The fruit of the Spirit is love, joy, peace, patience, kindness, goodness, faithfulness, gentleness and self-control. Against such things there is no law"* (Galatians 5:22,23). God has given us His Spirit, so we can obey whatever He commands, living the kind of life that pleases Him.

This will mean some struggle in our lives, as we subdue our former way of living to our new way of living in the Spirit. *"So I say, live by the Spirit, and you will not gratify the desires of the sinful nature. For the sinful nature desires what is contrary to the Spirit, and the Spirit what is contrary to the sinful nature. They are in conflict with each other, so that you do not do what you want"* (Galatians 5:16,17). You are at war, with your very self as the battleground. No matter how hard it gets, however, if you continue to live by the Spirit, *the Spirit is going to win.*

God gives us His Spirit for more than the conquest of our personal lives. God has a whole world to win. Just before Jesus ascended into heaven, He announced His world-conquering mission to His disciples: *"All authority in heaven and on earth has been given to me. Therefore go and make disciples of all nations, baptizing them in the name of the Father and of the Son and of the Holy Spirit, teaching them to obey everything I have commanded you"* (Matthew 28:18, 19).

Make disciples (followers) of all nations? Sounds impossible! But Jesus explained the secret of our success: *"And surely I will be with you always, to the very end of the age"* (Matthew 28:20). Jesus Himself is with His ambassadors by His Spirit. He guarantees their witness to the nations will be successful. He promised: *"You will receive power when the Holy Spirit comes on you; and you will be my witnesses in Jerusalem, and in all Judea and Samaria, and to the ends of the earth"* (Acts 1:8).

Since that day, the witness to Jesus Christ has spread to all the nations. Jesus is true to His promise. By His Spirit, He remains with His people in their witnessing for Him, enabling them to fulfill His command to bring salvation to the ends of the earth.

Using the term *water* as a symbol of the *Holy Spirit,* Jesus declared: ***"If a man is thirsty, let him come to me and drink. Whoever believes in me, as the Scripture has said, streams of living water will flow from within him"*** (John 7:37,38). The Spirit, dwelling within the people of God, feeds and refreshes us, then flows out from us to all the world, bringing life and health to all the nations. Jesus described the gift of the Spirit to the church as being ***"clothed with power from on high"*** (Luke 24:49). We have the power to win!

> ***Since we live by the Spirit, let us keep in step with the Spirit"*** (Galatians 5:25).

When we keep in step with the Holy Spirit by doing what He commands in His Word, we have power to meet all life's problems without being defeated.

The Holy Spirit, the enabling power of God, is God's rich gift to His children. Jesus says He will guide us into all truth.

Becoming a Christian doesn't make your problems disappear, but does bring them into focus. As the Bible helps your love and understanding grow, you become confident in the fact that God has solutions for your every problem. Watching His creative solutions to your problems actually increases your joy in being a Christian.

Your Christian growth gives glory to God. As you deal with the problems of life, you observe their tremendous potential for actually giving glory to Him!

Thus, every problem can bring you new *power for living.*

Your word is a lamp to my feet
and a light for my path.
Psalm 119:105

HOW TO
READ
THE BIBLE

Suppose you are planning a trip. You carefully pack your suitcase, perhaps suspend newspaper delivery. You attend to every necessary detail except one: you neglect to get a map.

Because you're in a hurry to reach your destination, you jump in the car and start driving. North, south, east, west? Which direction do you choose?

Since you feel you're going the right way, you keep driving. Suddenly, however, you feel tired and stop to get something to drink. You notice a sign which gives the name of a state—not the state for which you are headed. All that time spent driving, and so little to show for it!

Of course, in real life you wouldn't put yourself in such a foolish situation, would you? You'd have enough sense to use a map and make the most of your travel time.

Unfortunately, when it comes to something of such extreme importance as studying the Bible, many people adopt a hit-or-miss attitude. They don't take the Bible seriously enough. They're so intent on reaching the destination —finding God's will for their life or the solution to a certain problem—that they ignore the basic steps they should take. In other words, they ignore the fundamental Instruction Manual, the Word of God which has the principles by which we live and die.

Some people fail to read the Bible because they feel they haven't had special training. The fact is, the Bible was written to *everyone,* regardless of educational background or social status.

Another reason people don't read the Bible when they know they should is because they may not want to be brought up short by its message. The Word of God is described as a two-edged sword, piercing to the deepest levels of our being and revealing the thoughts and intents of the heart. No wonder we may want to avoid reading the Bible. Still, as Christians, we are commanded to read it.

WHEN EVERYTHING ELSE FAILS...

Life is similar to the "travel story." So often we stumble through life without reading the instructions. We try to solve our problems through every conceivable way except the obvious. Remember that old saying, "When everything else fails, *read the directions."* It's true. If we would just read the instructions to life, we would find out how it should work.

God gave us those instructions a long time ago, in the Bible. Everything you need to know regarding family, work, money, fear, pain, and many other topics, is there. Any problem you experience has a solution in the Bible. (We covered some of them in an earlier chapter.)

St. Paul refers to the Bible, the Word of God, as the "Sword of the Spirit" and none of life's problems can resist His sharp sword. All we have to do is read the instructions.

There is another parallel between the travel story and life. Many Christians fear they won't understand the Bible, so they don't read and study the Scriptures. They attend church and Sunday school class, perhaps even attend a casual Bible study every now and then. Perhaps they once tried to read the Bible, but had trouble comprehending it.

For them, instructions to life remain a closed book. What's the problem? People don't know *how to read* the Bible. They're convinced they've failed in many ways! They need to read the instructions. *But they just don't know how.*

THE A, B, Cs OF BIBLE READING

To best read and study the Bible, you need some general guidelines. Imagine the first day in art class. The teacher takes the students downtown to a large art museum. The group pauses in front of an interesting picture whose meaning totally escapes them. The teacher starts talking about the picture. She overwhelms the students with numerous facts about the picture. One of the students, listening in amazement, said, "How do you do it?"

The teacher tells them, "You first need to know something about the artist—when and where he lived, and what he tried to express through his art. Then you should understand something about his style. Every artist has his own way of depicting his ideas. He uses many kinds of techniques."

Finally, the teacher says, "You must know the mechanics of painting—composition, shadow and light, color, and proportion." The same ideas apply to studying the Bible.

Know the Author

Studying the Bible is much like learning to interpret art. First, you should know the Author. There's the story of a lady who went to a bookstore to buy an interesting book she heard about. When she took it home and tried to read it, she discovered it was too hard to understand. One day she met the author of the book at a party. They fell in love and eventually married. She learned that once she knew the author, she could understand what he was saying in his book.

Before you can understand the Bible, you have to know the Author in the person of Jesus Christ. The God of the Bible is a Person. You get to know Him by acknowledging that you deserve His punishment, because you have sinned against Him. And then you must rest and rely on Him with all your heart and life. Such trust is called faith.

Once you know God through Jesus Christ, you'll have the most important thing you need to study the Bible. It is called *hunger for God's Word.* This hunger is a sign of health. People who are not hungry are usually not too healthy. It's the same way with God's food. You should have a hunger for God's Word. Your study of it will be in proportion to your hunger. The Psalmist in the Bible said, ***"How sweet are your promises to my taste, sweeter than honey to my mouth"*** (Psalm 119:103).

Your hunger is dependent on your relationship with God. If you lack hunger it's because you don't know Him, or there is something wrong with your relationship.

How God Says Things

Although there are sixty-six books in the Bible, it is only *one* book. So, there is just one Author. You'll find, though the style of its human authors varies, God uses a basic pattern in communicating to man. First, He gives a command or a promise. Second, the Bible tells of man's response. Third, a word of evaluation is given.

This simple pattern repeats itself throughout the Bible. Regardless of the literature, it's there, if you look. Let's take a few examples. At the very beginning of the Bible, God creates the world with His Word. God then tells man to take care of the world (garden) He has created (Genesis 2:15). God said that Adam's faithfulness would be rewarded with eternal life (verse 17). This is the command/promise. Adam is commanded to do something, and a promise is given in relationship to that command. The promise is not always given right after the command, and sometimes the promise is given and the command is implied.

After the command/promise we read about Adam's and also Eve's response. Adam starts off well. He names his new wife (Genesis 2:19-25), then sets out together with her to do what God told him to do. That is the right kind of response.

But in chapter three, another response to God's command/promise is seen. Satan, in the form of a serpent, tempts Adam and Eve to disobey God's command/promise. In fact, Satan substitutes a new command/promise. He says, *"Do what God told you not to do, and you will be like the gods"* (Genesis 3:4).

Satan's command was to break God's command. That's always Satan's temptation. And his promise was something that could never happen on such terms. Adam and Eve were creatures, made of dust. God has no beginning and no end. He was their Creator. The creature can never be the Creator. Like Satan's command, Satan's promise is hollow. He offers what can never be, if you do it his way.

Adam and Eve listened to Satan's command/promise. They sinned. For the first time guilt was experienced. Every means to cover this guilt was exhausted. They tried to hide from God. They tried to cover up their sin. But Adam and Eve stood exposed before God. Maybe they could cover it up before the world around them. But they could never do this with God. This was man's *response* as recorded in Genesis 3:1-8.

In the remainder of Genesis three we see the evaluation of God. The *evaluation* comes in a process of judgment that begins with several questions (verses 9-13). God makes man condemn himself, and you get the impression that Adam and Eve are in court, God's court. And this process of evaluation/judgment is man's accounting for his actions.

After Adam and Eve passed the buck, God passed His judgment (verses 14-19). Man failed by his fall. He was unable to stand up under God's evaluation. But God's evaluation/judgment did not stop here.

The end of the chapter tells how God transferred His judgment by killing the animals and covering with their skins the nakedness of man. This was God's evaluation/judgment.

Command/promise, response, and evaluation/judgment —this threefold pattern appears everywhere in the Bible. Let's go to the end of the Bible into the New Testament.

In Paul's letters, or epistles, the same pattern is used. He generally begins with something called a *salutation.* Often he might change the pattern a little. At the beginning he might tell of how they have responded to God's *command/ promises.* But then, he goes into the specific commands and promises they are to keep.

Sometimes Paul just reminds them. Finally, he gives an evaluation/judgment because he speaks for God.

If Paul feels really upset with a particular church, such as the one at Corinth, Greece, he starts out giving them an evaluation/judgment. But the pattern is always there.

If you think a moment, you recognize the basic pattern of history. History begins, literally, with God's Word. By that Word, He creates the world. Man's response is to throw away that Word. Then God comes in history to evaluate man.

The first time God came to the world was at the Incarnation, when God became man in the Person of Jesus. But Jesus' brief ministry mainly allowed Him to retell God's Word to man. Jesus said, ***"Do not think that I have come to abolish the Law or the Prophets; I have not come to abolish them but to fulfill them"*** (Matthew 5:17). So, Jesus did not want to judge the world in His first coming (John 12:47).

At the end of His ministry, He faced the evaluation/judgment of God for man. He was sentenced to die on a cross because the penalty was death (Romans 6:23). But that was not the end of history. Man has been given a reprieve. He is allowed more time to respond to God's commands and promises. The end of history is promised. It will end with God's final evaluation/judgment. The end occurs when Christ comes again.

So, history follows the same pattern. If you look closely, you'll see the same basic command/promises, responses, and evaluation/judgments that we pointed out in the early chapters of Genesis. This brings us to the next general guideline for reading the Bible.

Where to Begin

In introducing a novice to God, and to His Son, Jesus Christ, many Christians believe the newcomer should read the Gospel of John before any other part of the Bible. This book is the Apostle John's witness of Christ. It was written with inspired eloquence and power by Jesus's special friend, John, known as "the beloved disciple."

John was one of Jesus' twelve apostles. Like the other writers of the books of the New Testament, John probably wrote his gospel only a few years after the Ascension of Jesus to heaven. He knew Jesus personally and recounted the events recorded in his gospel as an eyewitness.

John's purpose is not primarily to present a detailed history of Jesus' three years of ministry, nor is it to give us a personal portrait of Jesus Christ. Rather, John tells us that he has written *"that you may believe that Jesus is the Christ, the Son of God, and that by believing you may have life in his name"* (John 20:31).

Other believers argue for beginning one's Bible reading with the Gospel of Matthew—the beginning of the New Testament. Query a Bible scholar, however, or anyone else who loves and enjoys God's Word, and you will become convinced that you need both Old and New Testaments, in sequence. One illuminates the other. Each contains formidable power for living.

Eventually you will want to begin at the beginning. Some people try to read the Bible backwards, and it is possible to understand many things about the Bible when you do this. Like any other book, however, it is better to read it as the Author wrote it. You might think of it this way: Genesis is the first chapter, and Revelation is the last chapter of the Book God has given man.

"But," you protest, "what about those first books of the Bible? I heard they're pretty difficult to understand, and don't have much to do with me." Please stay tuned for further guidelines for studying the Bible!

Scripture with Scripture

A famous preacher once said, "If you don't understand something in the Bible, keep reading. God will clear it up somewhere else in His Word." That preacher was really saying three things.

One, read the entire Bible. God gave us sixty-six books of Scripture. Read them all. The Bible hangs together with the same basic threefold pattern discussed earlier. So you can go to other places within the Bible for help.

Two, remember that the Bible is its own authority. There is no other book above the Bible. You don't need to go any place else except the Bible itself to understand its meaning. So, use Scripture to understand (interpret) other Scripture. This is probably the most important rule in interpreting the Bible.

Someone may tell you that so-and-so says the Bible means this or that. If he is right, it's because the Scriptures themselves have already said it. That is why a good cross reference system is very helpful. Some Bibles have Scripture *references* in the margins. These are called *cross references.* They probably refer to other uses of the words or ideas.

By looking at how a word or an idea is used somewhere else, you can begin to see what it means. For example, let's say you are reading in the Book of Leviticus about all of the laws concerning blood sacrifice. You're not sure how all that relates to you so you follow up some cross references on "blood." Then you discover that blood is very important in the Bible.

Maybe you even remember the basic threefold pattern. Remember, God's evaluation/judgment of Adam and Eve involved the provision of animal skins. That meant the shedding of blood. So then you see that this book is part of God's provision for God's people to cover their sin.

But if you don't remember that much, you'll at least discover that the most important blood in the world was shed on the cross. If you see that, you can interpret the blood in Leviticus with the blood of Jesus. You'll start to learn a lot about Jesus's death by looking at the death required of many animals in Leviticus.

Three, use Scripture you can clearly understand to interpret those parts that are not so clear to you. It's pretty hard to understand the Bible when you use obscure passages. If you work from the clear to the unclear, however, you'll be able to acquire a general understanding of almost anything.

Obviously you won't be able to understand everything perfectly. The Bible is an inexhaustible Book. Augustine, a great man of God, wrote in a letter to his son in A.D. 412 concerning the inexhaustibility of the Bible. He said, "Such is the depth of the Christian Scriptures that even if I were attempting to study them and nothing else from early boyhood to decrepit old age, with the utmost leisure, the most unwearied zeal, and talents greater than I have, I would still daily be making progress in discovering their treasures." So, don't be frustrated that you cannot understand everything.

Remember what the art teacher said to her art class? Two of the guidelines she gave have been applied under the *A, B, Cs of the Bible.* But she also said that it was important to study something about painting if you really want to be able to interpret well. In the same way, if you really want to do more serious reading of the Bible, you need to look at a *definite method* for studying it.

THE THREE Rs

Now we are ready to step up from the *A,B,Cs* to the *three Rs,* which is a basic method to follow. It is a method that's simple, yet satisfying. The three Rs are *read, record, and respond.*

READ

The best way to begin is to read and reread the Bible. Maybe a discussion on *reading* suprises you, but that's the finest way to study the Bible. Someone once said, "We've done everything to the Bible. Now all we need to do is read it."

Read for the Big Picture

The first time you read a book in the Bible, try to get an overall feel for what the book says. This is the *skyscraper view*. Don't worry about details, but try to get a panoramic sweep. It's like climbing into a tree to see everything from above.

In the early days of flying, a famous pilot lost one of his most valuable instruments during a flight. He saw it land in a dense field below. He landed his plane near by and began to look for the instrument. The field was thicker than he thought, and he could not find it, but he remembered he could see it from the air. All the pilot needed was something from which to get his bearings. He took off his coat and laid it in the field. Then he flew his plane into the sky, where he could see both the instrument and the coat. This perspective enabled the pilot to land and find the instrument without any difficulty.

As you read the Bible for the big picture, you pick up the *context*. That is like the pilot's coat. The context sets your bearings. When you know generally what the Author means, the parts make more sense. Without context, the parts can become scrambled.

Besides that, it's possible to make some bad mistakes in studying the Bible. The Scriptures have been used to prove almost anything. But if you study the Bible to submit your mind to the mind of the Author, the Word of God can only say what the Author intended. Remember, therefore, *a text without a context is a pretext.*

To help you get a handle on the big picture, try titling each chapter. When you finish, put all the chapters together and title the book. You may end up going back to change a few of the titles. That's all right. At this point, you're putting your first impressions into the titles. You'll be surprised at the accuracy of first impressions.

Read for the Details

Bible study should not stop at first impressions, just as we should not stop there when getting to know a person. After all, first impressions can be wrong. So, now you need to become more intent, and move from the skyscraper to the ground level. Let's take the *microscopic view.* At this point, the following steps can help.

One, title each paragraph. A paragraph is the basic unit of study. It represents one basic thought in the author's mind. A good translation like the *New International Version* breaks up the text into paragraphs. Read each paragraph and try to come up with a simple title.

Two, ask questions. One day a man was having pains in his stomach, and ended up in the doctor's office. The doctor began to ask him several questions. "Where does it hurt?" "How often does the pain come?" "What kind of pain is it?" "Does food relieve the pain?" Eventually the doctor asked more than one hundred questions. That process enabled the doctor to determine why the man's stomach was hurting.

Bible study is much the same. You need to ask questions about the Bible text. Simply ask: Who? What? When? Where? Why? Use each chapter and paragraph to guide your study. Work through the chapters, asking these questions.

Begin with the question *who.* Make sure you know the author of the book. Also, note *who* is speaking. Some books of the Bible contain many conversations. It is very important to know who is talking—especially when it may be Jesus!

The other questions are important too. Know *when* something is happening. Follow the locations geographically, and study *where* something is taking place. And finally, ask the question *why.* "Why is this chapter here and not some other place in the Bible?" God put it there and not somewhere else for a reason. You may have to go to other portions of the Bible to answer that question. Go ahead. You'll find many answers to other questions. And don't be frustrated if your study raises more questions than you can answer.

Three, use some Bible study tools. Asking questions is fun, but there comes a time when you want some answers. There are several tools that can help you in your study.

First, *concordances.* A concordance is an invaluable Bible study tool that lists all of the references of each word in the Bible.

For example, let's say you wanted to look up the word *love.* A concordance lists all of the places the word is used. By looking at the ways "love" is used, you can determine what it means in your text under study. Two good concordances are *Young's Analytical Concordance,* and *Cruden's Complete Concordance. Young's* allows you to trace a word back to its original Hebrew and Greek usage. The Old Testament was written in Hebrew, and the New Testament was written in Greek. *Cruden's* is just for the English text, but it's a very good concordance.

One final suggestion on concordances. Make sure you find out what translation of the Bible a concordance goes with. The ones referred to above reference the *King James Version.*

Second, *Bible dictionaries.* A Bible dictionary is like an English dictionary. It is a collection of articles that explains works, places, people, and other subjects in the Bible. One of the best Bible dictionaries is the *New Bible Dictionary.*

Third, *commentaries.* A commentary is a running explanation of the Bible text itself. Perhaps you are studying the first chapter of the Gospel of John. A commentary would give you an explanation of each verse. A fine one-volume Bible commentary preferred by many is the *New Bible Commentary.*

Many other tools are available to a serious Bible student. But these are the main ones. You can find them at any bookstore which sells Christian literature.

Begin with these books, which can help you answer many questions which will surface in your study. A list of books is included in the section titled "For Further Reading."

Look for Things that are Alike

The mind notices and remembers things that are alike. If we see two dresses alike, among many others, we tend to remember them. Twins stick out in our mind. And a child will notice another toy that is just like his.

Bible books contain many internal similarities. In the 15th chapter of the Gospel of Luke, the author mentions three stories in which there is rejoicing over the lost being found. These stories obviously have things in them that are alike. By taking note of this, the Bible student can learn about the message of the author.

Look for Things that are Different

We also notice differences. A tall man stands out next to a midget. Red contrasts against a white background. Life is full of contrasts. They leave impressions on our minds.

In one of the Gospel stories, two men respond to God. One says, "God, please be merciful to me because I am a sinner." The other one turns up his nose at God. To notice this contrast is just as helpful as observing things that are alike. The contrast displays the author's overall thrust.

Look for Things Repeated

Imagine a young woman writing from a trip to the lake about some of the things she did. She writes that on Saturday she went horseback riding with Jim. On Sunday she visited a nearby church with Jim. On Monday, she attended a movie with Jim. On and on she writes, continually mentioning Jim in connection with everything she did. At the end of her letter, she says, "P.S., I am not at all interested in Jim." Would you believe her? Why not?

She continually *repeats* that everything was done with Jim. In fact, she did very little without him. She made a point, whether she intended to or not.

In God's Word, we find the same. Psalm 118: 1-4 repeats a phrase, ***"And His love endures forever."*** The Psalmist desired to make a point. He does so by repetition. The Bible will do this in many ways. God is revealing His Word. He wants to emphasize and de-emphasize things by repeating things about Himself. Watch for these repetitions.

Reading the Bible can involve you as much as you wish. The methods already discussed will help you to read carefully. Reading is not enough, however, if you want to study the Bible. Your mind will forget. It will function better if you'll do something else while you read.

RECORD

Write down everything you do in your study of the Scriptures. Questions, comments, observations, passing thoughts, charts, pictures, diagrams, and anything else should go down on paper. Writing does something for the mind. The movement of the pencil jars thoughts out.

Don't worry about writing something someone else may consider silly. It may help you to understand something very important in the Bible. After all, that's more important, isn't it?

Feel free to write in the margins of your Bible. Many great men and women of God take notes in their Bibles. When one Bible is full of notes, they go to another. They've learned that writing helps to open up the mind.

Why not start a little notebook of your Bible study time? This will help you better to organize your reading. It also will preserve your notes. Perhaps someone will use your Bible study notes to teach a Sunday school lesson, perhaps you'll someday teach a class.

You also might want to record your personal *paraphrase* of the passage being studied. A paraphrase is a rewriting of Scripture in your own words.

You'll be astonished at the results of your paraphrase. It will make you study aspects of the verse of which you weren't aware. Also, it will help you remember what the passage says. Third, it forces you to understand the passage better.

From reading to recording, you now know how to read through the Bible and write down what you learn. But this is still not enough. Unless you do one more step, your Bible study falls short.

RESPOND

Bible study is not the end. It is the means to an end. God calls you to walk in His light (I John 1:5). He wants you to obey His commandments (I John 2:4). Bible study, therefore, is for this end. After you've studied, God wants you to respond. How? Think in terms of *application.*

Your study will uncover many things God wants you to do. In your relation to God, ask yourself what the passage teaches you about fellowship to enjoy, commands to obey, promises to claim, and prayers to express.

In relation to yourself, the Scriptures provide a new perspective on your past background and heritage. Present experiences take different focus. Your values, priorities, and standards will be addressed by Scripture.

Then there is your relationship to others. Home, church, society, and the world, are categories that God changes. His Word tells you how these areas are to be ordered.

Finally, your relation to our Enemy, Satan, changes. You learn to resist him. The Bible is a guidebook to the devices Satan uses. You will see sins to avoid. God provides armor to wear. He wants you to put it on and fight the battle, and build His Kingdom.

These applications will be found in the Word of God. He wants you to respond to His Word. Specifically, you can begin by *confessing* sin.

Next, respond in *faith.* Ask God in prayer to build what you are studying into your life.

Lastly, *obey* Him.

Obedience is the way we show God that we love Him.

THE WHOLE POINT

Someone has said the Bible is like a roaring lion. It need not be defended, simply turn it loose. When you read and study the Bible with a concluding response of obedience, you turn the Bible loose in your life and your world. This is what man was created to do. By His Word, God made the world. By His Word He put breath into man (Genesis 2:7). You were made for His Word. So, turn it loose in your life!

And God said,
Let us make man in our ima
after our likeness:
and let them have domini
over the fish of the sea,
and over the fowl of the a
and over the cattle,
and over all the earth,
and over every creeping th
that creepeth upon the ear
Genesis 1:26

GOD'S PERSPECTIVE

One result of turning the Bible loose in your life is that you will find yourself meditating on it. It will also become part of you, very much like a nourishing rainfall that soaks into the ground. You will find its truths becoming a part of you, since God's Spirit is constantly working inside of you.

NEW HEART AND MIND

When someone becomes a Christian, several things happen. He becomes a new person with a new heart and mind. God says, *"I will give you a new mind and put a new heart within you"* (Ezekiel 36:26).

The new heart—the center of your being—gives life to an otherwise dead person (Ephesians 2:1). The life imparted through this *"new birth"* makes it possible for the once spiritually blind man to see the things of God (John 3:3). Prior to the new birth, Satan—the *"god of this world"* had blinded the unbelieving man (II Corinthians 4:4).

The mind also undergoes a radical change and must continue to be renewed by not being conformed to the world's way of thinking (Romans 12:2). This means that old ways of thinking (man-centered ways of thinking) must be *"put off"* and new ways of thinking (God-centered ways of thinking) must be *"put on"* (Ephesians 4:17-24). The mind must be trained in biblical thinking so that the Christian will be able *"to discern good and evil"* (Hebrews 5:14). If the Christian does not begin with God in his thinking process, we can be sure he will not come to God's conclusions about the way he should act.

A NEW WORLD

When the Bible speaks on a subject, it is every Christian's duty to study the topic and act upon the Bible's commands. Paul declared he did not hesitate to proclaim *"the whole will of God"* (Acts 20:27). A quick survey of the Bible will reveal some of its wide-ranging subject matter which makes up the will of God for us.

The Bible speaks about:

history (Matthew 24; Hebrews 13:8)

economics (Leviticus 25:35-38; Deuteronomy 8:18)

education (Deuteronomy 6:4-9)

geography (Nehemiah 9:6; Acts 17:26)

political science (Romans 13:1-7)

administration (Exodus 18:13-27)

the military (Deuteronomy 20)

leadership (Proverbs 28:2; 29:8)

social relationships (Luke 10:30-37; I Corinthians 13)

social problems (Isaiah 1:1-23; Ezekiel 16:49 50)

marriage (Genesis 2:23,24; Matthew 19:5)

family (Ephesians 5:22-6:4)

property (Exodus 20:15)

law (Exodus 20-23:9), and so on

WHAT IS A WORLD VIEW?

Ideas have consequences. What you *think* about God, yourself, and your world determines how you *live* in relation to God, yourself, and your world.

Ideas form the basis of a person's *world view.* But what is a world view? "Your world view, of course, is how you view the world. It is the set of presuppositions—that which is believed beforehand—which underlies all of our decisions and actions. These presuppositions (our world view) determine our thinking patterns, which in turn influence our actions. ...Our world view may be conscious or unconscious, but it determines our destiny and the destiny of the society we live in" (Ron Jenson, *Together We Can Deal with Life in the 80's,* p. 27f).

A world view is simply the way you look at yourself and the world around you. It includes what you think about God, yourself, your neighbors, your family, civil government, the arts, economics, morality, business, and every other area of life.

If you were to ask a person's opinion about himself or something he does you would then learn his views on these subjects. This type of examination could continue until every conceivable aspect of an individual's life was examined. At the conclusion of the questioning you would, in fact, have a pretty accurate picture of his world view.

Some people have more developed world views than others, but everybody has a world view, no matter how limited it might be. In fact the Bible assures us that the meaning we give to ourselves and our world, seen and unseen, originates within our own mind: ***"For as [a man] thinks within himself, so he is"*** (Proverbs 23:7).

If you believe you are a created being responsible to

your Creator for all things, then your world view will be constructed around the principle that you are dependent upon God for a proper understanding of the world. If, however, you believe that you are an independent, highly evolved animal, dependent upon no person or no thing, then your world view will reflect this self-centeredness. Your world view will reflect man's glory instead of God's.

AT THE BEGINNING

The idea of a world view is not new. God interpreted the world for Adam and Eve. God's Word was to be the starting point in their understanding of a proper (biblical) world view.

Even though Adam and Eve were morally perfect, they did not have complete knowledge about God, themselves, and their world. They had to depend continually upon God as the source of knowledge and understanding: *"The fear of the Lord is the beginning of knowledge, but fools despise wisdom and discipline"* (Proverbs 1:7).

God's understanding of Himself and the creation is *independent* and *complete*. There is nothing outside of God that He must depend on to know and there is nothing that God does not already know. Man's knowledge, however, is *dependent* and *limited*. Without God as the source and interpreter of knowledge, man would know nothing.

It is in God's light that we see light (Psalm 36:9). The Apostle Paul affirms God's *independent* and *complete* knowledge by saying that in Christ *"are hidden all the treasures of wisdom and knowledge"* (Colossians 2:3). If you truly want to know, you must understand it is God who teaches you knowledge (Psalm 94:10).

Satan's purpose in overturning God's moral order was to

The earth is the Lord's,
and everything in it,
the world, and all who live in it;
for he founded it upon the seas
and established it upon the waters.
Psalm 24:1,2

convince Adam and Eve that God's view of the world was only one view among many. In persuading Eve to eat of the tree of the knowledge of good and evil, Satan was, in effect, tempting her to develop an *independent* world view in competition with God's: *"You will be like God, knowing good and evil"* (Genesis 3:5). The temptation was not over a piece of fruit. Instead, it was a struggle over who would be the interpreter of all reality.

OBSTACLES TO BUILDING A BIBLICAL WORLD VIEW

The building of a reliable and complete biblical world view cannot be accomplished immediately. False views of reality must be replaced with a biblical view of reality: *"So I tell you this, and insist on it in the Lord, that you must no longer live as the Gentiles do, in the futility of their thinking. They are darkened in their understanding and separated from the life of God because of the ignorance that is in them due to the hardening of their hearts"* (Ephesians 4:17,18).

A world view constructed on the belief that man is the center of life, interpreting all reality independent of God, is a shaky one at best. If everyone interprets reality independent of God, our world will continue its downhill slide to destruction.

If man creates the standard for what is right and wrong, he is really saying, "I am god. What I say goes." That kind of thinking is a subtle form of atheism. The Bible says that the fool says in his heart, "There is no God." And the result of that type of thinking is death—spiritual, moral, physical, and social death: *"All who hate [God's wisdom] love death"* (Proverbs 8:36).

In a recent speech Alexander Solzhenitsyn, the exiled Russian author, warned that "the entire 20th century is being sucked into the vortex of atheism and self-destruction." The only thing that can stop the whirlpool is our returning to God and His view of the world. He said, "We can only reach out with determination for the warm hand of God, which we have so rashly and self-confidently pushed away."

A CORRECTIVE LENS

Developing a biblical world view never can be separated from Jesus' saving work. If men and women do not turn to Jesus Christ as Saviour and Lord, they will turn to themselves, another individual, an idea, a movement, or a political system. Our choice of "Saviour" will determine how our world will be structured.

For many, the Bible is only a book that imparts "spiritual" truth but has very little to say about "secular" matters. Actually the Bible does not divide life between sacred and secular or spiritual and material levels of reality (Colossians 2:16-23). A real division, however, does exist between:

good and evil (Hebrews 5:14),

obedience and disobedience (II Corinthians 10:5,6), and

faith and faithlessness (Matthew 21:21).

When you commit your life to God through Jesus Christ, that includes all your relationships. Everything should be affected:

family affairs (Ephesians 5:22-6:1-4),

personal economic matters (Romans 13:8),

personal relationships (Galatians 5:18-24),

sinful habits (Ephesians 5:25-32),

judicial decisions (I Corinthians 6:1-11),

eating and drinking (I Corinthians 10:31),

business dealings (I Thessalonians 4:6),

church discipline (Matthew 18:15-20),

education (Ephesians 6:4),

civil affairs (I Peter 2:13-17), and so on.

A biblical world view sees all of life through the "corrective lens" of Scripture, recognizing that *"the man without the Spirit does not accept the things that come from God for they are foolishness to him, and he cannot understand them, because they are spiritually discerned"* (I Corinthians 2:14).

The only true world view is God's view of the world. Christians have been given "the mind of Christ" which enables them to think God's thoughts *after* Him: *"The spiritual man makes judgments about all things, but he himself is not subject to any man's judgment: 'For who has known the mind of the Lord that he may instruct him?' But we have the mind of Christ"* (I Corinthians 2:15-16).

The Word of God is the standard of authority before which all other standards of authority must bow. Experience, the consensus of the majority, tradition, or circumstances cannot be used as standards of authority for developing a consistently biblical world view.

God's Word will give us the mind of Christ because it is *"perfect"* (Psalm 19:7), *"forever"* (Isaiah 40:8), *"trustworthy"* (Psalm 93:5), *"sacred"* (Proverbs 30:6), a *"light"* (Psalm 19:8), *"fire"* (Jeremiah 23:29), a *"crushing hammer"* (Jeremiah 23:29), *"living"* (Hebrews 4:12), and will never fail to accomplish its stated purpose (Isaiah 55:8-11). The word of man is feeble and fallible, and cannot be trusted to evaluate life in all its fulness: *"Stop trusting in man, who has but a breath in his nostrils. Of what account is he?"* (Isaiah 2:22).

In very practical terms, having "the mind of Christ" helps us to see the world through God's eyes, as it were. Of course as finite (limited) human beings, we can never (nor should we) hope to have unlimited knowledge. God would have us trust Him by obeying the Word He has given us.

Every area of life must be reached with the good news of God's love and forgiveness. This means making an impact on the world around you—in whatever areas of life show signs of moral decay:

government
entertainment
education
sports
business
law

and so on.

The task is great, but we have been promised that we have not been left alone to accomplish the task. Jesus said, *"I will never leave you or forsake you."* And He always keeps His word.

SUMMING IT UP

We've covered a lot of material in this book. It's purpose was to introduce you to **POWER FOR LIVING.** That power is Jesus Christ. All the power we need for living is found in Him. Jesus came to give us life, an abundant life. But the abundant life comes through acknowledging our sin, turning our backs on it, and turning to Jesus Christ in faith. There is no possible way that we can muster up enough power from within ourselves to get right with God. God demands perfection. The breaking of just one commandment is enough to put us under the condemnation of God.

God has not left us under judgment, however. He sent His Son Jesus Christ to pay the penalty for our sins. All the righteous judgment that God could have poured out on us He poured out on Jesus: *"He was pierced for our transgressions, he was crushed for our iniquities; the punishment that brought us peace was upon him, and by his wounds we are healed"* (Isaiah 53:5).

This is true **POWER FOR LIVING.** Those who are in Christ are no longer under the condemnation of God. Through Jesus *"we have peace with God"* (Romans 5:1).

This power is not yours unless you come to Christ. The promises Jesus makes cannot be yours until you surrender all your pride and self-centeredness and embrace Jesus Christ as your Lord and Saviour. There is no other way that life can be lived to its fullest without Him.

Power for living is yours when you surrender to Him.

Come to Christ.

Do it now!

*...I am with you always,
even unto the end of the world.*
Matthew 28: 20

BIBLE VERSIONS

King James Version (1611): The most well-known English version of the
Bible. Its literary quality is unsurpassed. We can hear its words
echoed in literature, poetry, hymns, and anthems.

New American Standard Version (1963): A modern translation of the
Bible that seeks to give a word for word rendering of the original
languages. An excellent study version of the Bible.

New King James (1982): An attempt by a team of 119 Bible translators to
retain the beauty and purity of the original *King James Version*
while making the text more readable.

New International Version (1978): A completely new translation of the
Bible made by over a hundred scholars. The distinguishing char-
acteristic of the *NIV* is its readability.

BIBLE HELPS

Every Christian should read the Bible in a systematic way every day. A
good place to start is with *The Daily Walk.* Each day you are given a
passage of Scripture to read with an overview of the passage's message.
A brief application to present-day circumstances follows the overview. By
following *The Daily Walk,* you will read the entire Bible in a year. A daily
devotional guide designed especially for families with a similar format is
called *Family Walk.* These can be ordered from Walk Thru the Bible
Ministries, P.O. Box 80587, Atlanta, GA 30366.

Adams, Jay E. *What to Do on Thursday.* Grand Rapids, MI: Baker Book
House, 1982. A handy guide on how to interpret and apply the
Bible to everyday living.

Alexander, David and Patricia Alexander. *Eerdmans' Handbook to the
Bible.* Grand Rapids, MI: Wm. B. Eerdmans Publishing Co., 1973.
A fully illustrated reference book that will help the reader under-
stand the Bible in its historical context.

Douglas, J. D. et al., eds. 2nd edition. *The New Bible Dictionary:
Revised.* Wheaton, IL: Tyndale House Publishers, Inc., 1982. A
comprehensive study of Bible words, theological topics, places,
people, names, etc.

Guthrie, Donald, et al., eds. *New Bible Commentary: Revised.* Grand
Rapids, MI: Wm. B. Eerdmans Publishing Co., 1970. A one-volume

commentary on the Bible put together by a team of scholars explaining every chapter in the Bible.

Strong, James. *The Exhaustive Concordance of the Bible.* Various publishers. Every word in the *King James Version* of the Bible is listed alphabetically with its corresponding verse. Hebrew and Greek dictionaries are included. A tremendous asset in locating forgotten verses.

Taylor, Kenneth. *The Living Bible.* Wheaton, IL: Tyndale House Publishers, 1971. This is a paraphrase of the Bible in everyday English. A paraphrast states in different language what he understands to be the original author's meaning. A paraphrase should never substitute for a translation.

Thomas, Robert L., et al., eds. *New American Standard Concordance of the Bible.* Nashville, TN: Holman Bible Publishers, 1981. A concordance based on the *New American Standard Version* of the Bible.

CHURCH HISTORY

Houghton, S. M. *Sketches from Church History.* Carlisle, PA: Banner of Truth Trust, 1980. A very readable and attractive historical presentation of how the Gospel of Jesus Christ affected the world.

Kuiper, B. K. *The Church in History.* Grand Rapids, MI: Wm. B. Eerdmans Publishing Co., 1964. Originally written as a textbook for Christian schools. Those unfamiliar with church history would do well to start with this book.

CHRISTIAN BELIEF

Blanchard, John. *Right With God.* Chicago, IL: Moody Press, 1971. A brief but thorough explanation of what it means to be a Christian.

Bridges, Jerry. *The Pursuit of Holiness.* Colorado Springs, CO: Navpress, 1978. Answers the basic questions that Christians have concerning their battle with sin.

Ferguson, Sinclair B. *Know Your Christian Life.* Downers Grove, IL: InterVarsity Press, 1981. A practical application of biblical doctrines.

LaHaye, Tim. *The Battle for the Mind.* Old Tappan, NJ: Fleming H. Revell Co., 1980. An explanation of the many ideas that influence us on a daily basis and shape our thinking.

CREDITS

BIBLE REFERENCES

With the exception of the following verses, all Scripture quotations are taken from the *Holy Bible: New International Version.* Copyright © 1978 New York International Bible Society. Used by permission from Zondervan Bible Publishers.

Page 40 — *The Living Bible,* copyrighted 1971 by Kenneth Taylor.

Page 129 — *The King James Version of the Bible* (1611).

TESTIMONIES

Appreciation to the following for permission to adapt material:

For Stan Smith, Roger Staubach, Chuck Colson — Printed by permission from *Evidence That Demands a Verdict* by Josh McDowell. Copyright © Here's Life Publishers, Inc., 1972, 1979. All rights reserved.

For Joe Greene and Julius Irving — Printed by permission from *Athletes in Action.* Copyright © Here's Life Publishers, Inc., 1981. All rights reserved.

For Wallace Johnson and Edward Johnson — Printed by permission from *Worldwide Challenge.* Copyright © Campus Crusade for Christ, Inc., 1978. All rights reserved.

OTHER SOURCES

Appreciation to Josh McDowell for permission to adapt material from his books, *Evidence That Demands a Verdict* and *Evidence Growth Guide: Part II* (Published by Here's Life Publishers, Inc., San Bernardino, California) and from *The Year of the Bible Official Reading Guide* © 1983 (Walk Thru the Bible Ministries, Atlanta, Georgia).

The Four Spiritual Laws appearing in Chapter 3 are printed by permission. © Campus Crusade for Christ, Inc., (1965). All rights reserved.

ILLUSTRATIONS

Opposite Title Page	*H. Armstrong Roberts.* Courtesy of H. Armstrong Roberts.
Opposite Contents	*J. Brignollo.* Courtesy of The Image Bank, Atlanta, Georgia.
Opposite Chapter One	*Gary Gladstone.* Courtesy of The Image Bank, Atlanta, Georgia.
Page 3	Courtesy of Campus Crusade for Christ, Inc.
Page 4	Courtesy of Campus Crusade for Christ, Inc.
Page 7	*ProServ, Inc.* Courtesy of Campus Crusade for Christ, Inc.
Page 8	Courtesy of Campus Crusade for Christ, Inc.
Page 11	*AIA Magazine.* Courtesy of Campus Crusade for Christ, Inc.
Page 12	Courtesy of the Arthur S. DeMoss Foundation.
Page 15	Courtesy of Campus Crusade for Christ, Inc.
Page 16	*AIA Magazine.* Courtesy of Campus Crusade for Christ, Inc.
Page 20	*H. Armstrong Roberts.* Courtesy of The Phelps Agency, Atlanta, Georgia.
Page 36	*Pete Turner.* Courtesy of The Image Bank, Atlanta, Georgia.
Page 40	*Peter Beney.* Courtesy of The Image Bank, Atlanta, Georgia.
Page 50	*H. Armstrong Roberts.* Courtesy of H. Armstrong Roberts.
Page 65	*B. Rauch.* Courtesy of The Image Bank, Atlanta, Georgia.
Page 68	*Richard Ustinich.* Courtesy of The Image Bank, Atlanta, Georgia.
Page 74	*Lisl Dennis.* Courtesy of The Image Bank, Atlanta, Georgia.
Page 88	*Gabe Palmer.* Courtesy of The Image Bank, Atlanta, Georgia
Page 91	*H. Armstrong Roberts.* Courtesy of H. Armstrong Roberts.
Page 94	*Larry Dale Gordon.* Courtesy of The Image Bank, Atlanta, Georgia.
Page 100	*B. Birzen.* Courtesy of The Image Bank, Atlanta, Georgia.
Page 118	*H. Sund.* Courtesy of The Image Bank, Atlanta Georgia.
Page 123	*Gabe Palmer.* Courtesy of The Image Bank, Atlanta, Georgia.
Page 129	*Stephen Frink.* Courtesy of The Image Bank, Atlanta, Georgia

ACKNOWLEDGMENTS

This book was commissioned by the Arthur S. DeMoss Foundation to celebrate *The Year of the Bible 1983*.

This book was produced by American Vision, P.O. Box 720515, Atlanta, Georgia 30328, with contributions from the following individuals:

Project Director. . . . . Steven R. Schiffman

Senior Editor. . . . . Victoria T. deVries

Editor. . . . . Charlotte Hale

Writers. . . . . David Chilton
Gary DeMar
Victoria T. deVries
Michael Gilstrap
Ray Sutton

Copyrights and Permission. . . . . . . Katherine A. Pletzke

Graphic Design. . . . . Deborah Willis Bruker